Over countless cups of coffee through the years, Mike has been a fount of encouragement and wisdom to me and Kristyn on many topics relating to Christ, His church, and His praise. It is our hope that this book will be the same deep resource, now shared with many.

Keith Getty, artist, hymn-writer, author of *Sing: How Worship Transforms Your Life, Family, and Church*

I really love and appreciate how Mike Harland seems to always understand how to help worship leaders, pastors, and churches get from point A to point B. He has a way of discerning what's going on in every church scenario and situation, and how to respond and move forward. No matter what your church or people group looks like, this read will encourage you, and will give you insight, perspective and vision. When someone loves the church like Mike loves the church, you can't help but be inspired and changed by their influence and wisdom.

Travis Cottrell, worship leader

Worship is too important not to talk about, but where do you start? Mike Harland offers a great place to begin that conversation. Not only do pastors and worship leaders need to work through this book, the entire congregation does. Mike has brought a great gift to the church.

Mike Glenn, senior pastor of Brentwood Baptist Church

Mike Harland gets it. The worship culture in the local church is critical for the fulfillment of the Great Commission, but the way many church leaders are navigating it is enabling batt the expense of winning the war for the glory of Christ and the multiplication of disciples. Pastors, musical worship leaders, and all other church leaders—read this book. The stakes are too high and the opportunity is too great for us to ignore this conversation.

Jim Shaddix, DMin., PhD, professor of Preaching, director of the Center for Preaching and Pastoral Leadership, Southeastern Baptist Theological Seminary , Wake Forest, North Carolina

Mike Harland is definitely one of the finest speakers I've ever heard, and a very close friend for many years. What Mike brings to the surface in *Worship Essentials* is absolute truth—worship is about the Jesus who really is, not the Jesus so many have created or imagined. This real Jesus is from the beginning the Word itself. He is absolutely the Way, the Truth, and the Life, not just another good guy, prophet, martyr, or whatever mankind has erroneously portrayed. As Mike declares so well, Jesus is real, consistent, present, and unchanging. He is the Jesus of the Bible. He is the only One worthy of our praise, adoration, thanksgiving, and worship. He holds the keys to life, death, and everything in between. Our only reasonable response to Jesus is to worship and serve Him, now and eternally. Read this book. Take the time to consider or reconsider your view of worship and Jesus—the real Jesus of the Bible. Pray for revelation of who He is, all He has done, and all He has promised to do. You won't be disappointed.

Stan Moser

Worship Essentials is a practical, down-to-earth exploration of four prerequisite values for any church seeking a healthy worship ministry. Mike Harland takes his gifts as a songwriter and masterfully communicates worship concepts—always telling a story, creatively interweaving narrative, skillfully closing chapters with a final hook line, purposely drawing the reader into personal relevance. This is a "MUST READ" resource for every pastor, worship pastor, worship team, and church leader. Mike provides honest, levelheaded, biblically-based advice for those seeking to lead worship that is free from agenda and the noisy clatter of self-promotion.

Vernon M. Whaley, DMin, DWS, PhD
dean of the Liberty University School of Music,
Lynchburg, Virginia

WORSHIP ESSENTIALS

GROWING A HEALTHY
WORSHIP MINISTRY
without
STARTING A WAR!

MIKE HARLAND

B&H
PUBLISHING GROUP
NASHVILLE, TENNESSEE

*To all the pastors, worship leaders, and believers
chasing hard after the heart of God in worship, and
for the rest of the world waiting on us to find it*

ACKNOWLEDGMENTS

The acknowledgments begin with my family, starting with my partner in life and ministry, my wife, Teresa, whose love and friendship are a constant source of encouragement; our kids, Lee and Jenna Harland, Elizabeth and Thomas Willis, and John Harland, along with Carolyn and Philip Stovall. They all make our house a place where joy abounds; also, my parents, Wiley and Martha Harland, who support me in prayer and have shaped so much of my life through a rich heritage of faith. Lastly, Madeleine and Caroline. Though you have not yet arrived, you already have my heart.

They continue with the pastors in my life: Jim Futral, Jim Shaddix, Mike Glenn, Dennis Worley, and Daniel Morris, who challenge me to love God's Word and make it the central part of my life.

They include the amazing team at LifeWay Worship that I am privileged to lead, and particularly our Leadership Team, Brian Brown, Craig Adams, Ricky King, Chasity Phillips, Renee Hardwick, and Vicki Dvoracek. They are the finest group of leaders I know, and I count them all as dear friends.

They must include Annaclaire Tadlock, my assistant, who brings order to chaos every day. This manuscript would not have happened without her help.

They also go to Thom Rainer and Eric Geiger; Dr. Rainer, for the opportunity to have the discussion about worship on his podcast with pastors that became the onus for this book, and Eric, whose leadership and accountability in my life helped craft the message found in these pages. These men have challenged me to grow beyond what I would have settled for without them.

The acknowledgments would be incomplete without mentioning the Life Group at Brentwood Baptist Church that I am blessed to lead, Once Delivered. These godly men and women challenge me to go deeper into God's Word every time we open the pages together. I am grateful for each one of them.

Finally, I have to include the team at B&H and particularly, Taylor Combs. His work on this project challenged me to be better and go harder after the goal. He is a true professional. I'm grateful for his patience and diligence on my behalf.

CONTENTS

VALUE FOUR: Aspire with Purpose

FOREWORD

I call him Guru.

I can't remember the first time I used that name to describe Mike Harland. It began as Worship Guru; most of the time now I abbreviate it to a single word.

As Mike notes in the introduction, he did not aspire to be called Guru, nor does he fully embrace the term. He has just come to accept it. Mike has been a regular feature of the podcast with Jonathan Howe and me, *Rainer on Leadership*. Those episodes are some of the most downloaded on the podcast.

Why is that? I'm glad you asked.

Mike Harland has that unique, if not uncanny, ability to speak both to the pastor and to the worship leader. He is a bridge to a chasm that exists in many churches. Simply said, when it comes to corporate worship, he gets it. He understands the challenges. He sees the opportunities. He embraces the possibilities. That is why pastors, worship leaders, and church members all seek his counsel. That is why he has a continuous flow of people who want to hear from him, who want to tell their stories and challenges, and who want some practical solutions to the issues so many church leaders and members face in corporate worship every week.

Such is the reason Mike is the Worship Guru.

It became apparent to me that Mike was meeting a huge need. He was and is connecting with church leaders, many of whom would have never thought they would seek the counsel of a worship leader. I saw it at LifeWay where we met and have worked together for thirteen years. I saw it on my podcast when the questions and comments would pour in after an episode released. I saw it on *Church Answers*, our resource where church leaders can ask questions 24/7.

So when Mike told me he was writing a book about many of the most important and pressing questions in corporate worship, my response was quick and blunt: *It's about time!*

You have before you one of the greatest resources a church leader could have. You will not see the worship services in your church the same again. You will not worship the same way again. It will be richer, deeper, and so much more understandable.

The book is called *Worship Essentials*. It is cliché and usually hyperbolic to say a book is destined to become a classic. But this book *should* become a classic. It's just that good. It's just that needed.

Get ready to take a journey where you will not return the same.

Get ready to grasp, embrace, and celebrate *Worship Essentials*.

Get ready to learn and hear from the Worship Guru.

You won't regret for one minute you bought this book and took this journey.

Thom S. Rainer
President and CEO of LifeWay Christian Resources

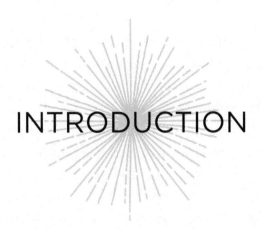

INTRODUCTION

It's a conversation I've had dozens of times. It usually starts something like this:

> **Church Pastor:** Mike, I've heard your guest appearances on Dr. Thom Rainer's podcast. I really need to talk to someone about our worship ministry and have a few questions. Have you got some time?
>
> **Me:** Happy to talk, pastor. Tell me about your church.

And for the next thirty minutes, this pastor will pour out his heart about the issues and challenges facing his church related to their worship ministry. To be clear, not every pastor is dealing with problems. In fact, some are serving in ministries with amazing opportunities and just want to explore a new strategy related to their corporate gatherings. But, in every case, a loving shepherd has called to ask questions about the worship and music experiences of the flock under his care.

Many pastors feel completely comfortable discussing the role of music in their church. But sometimes pastors avoid these kinds of conversations, especially if they feel unprepared or unqualified to discuss questions related to music.

Usually I start asking the questions. As I learn more and more about their history, their vision, their leadership, and their congregation, I explore with the pastor all of the kinds of expectations a church can have for worship ministry—some are realistic and well thought out. Some are unrealistic and impossible to measure.

You might wonder why I would be someone a pastor would call. I certainly don't see myself as an expert on these issues. It may be because I have been a fellow traveler on this journey for the last thirty-five years. I mostly believe it's because of the growing pressure pastors are feeling with this area of ministry.

Churches that are thought of as "successful" usually have corresponding worship ministries that are seen as effective and impacting. If a particular church is struggling, often the worship seems to be missing something. Pastors feel the urgency of addressing these questions because they understand the urgency of the times in which we live.

Many pastors that follow the podcast, *Rainer on Leadership*, have heard my dialogue with Dr. Rainer and realize their challenges in worship ministry are common to many others. Those discussions help them find a framework to examine the worship ministry of their church.

One pastor told me recently, "It's like you guys have been in my church. The questions and issues you have addressed are painfully apparent in our worship ministry right now." The truth is, I have found that many of the issues these pastors face are present to some degree in virtually every church.

That's why it was time to write this book.

Worship Essentials is an exploration of four necessary values for any church that hopes to have a healthy worship ministry. We also consider a biblical rationale of why these values are essential to the impact of those ministries.

I have made virtually every mistake a leader of a worship ministry can make and feel equipped to speak to the painful impact brought by an absence of these values. And, conversely, because I have had the privilege to be led well by great pastors and ministry leaders through the years, I also speak with confidence on the impact these values can have when they are in full bloom in a local church.

LifeWay Christian Resources has been an amazing place to invest this season of my life. Many more lessons have come through working with all kinds of churches and observing all kinds of worship cultures. Those ideas are certainly represented here as well.

One morning when I was going to the table for breakfast before leaving for the office, my wife asked me a funny question: "Well, what does the *Worship Guru* want for breakfast?" Her question gave away that she had been listening to *Rainer on Leadership*. In the previous episode that had just aired, Dr. Rainer tagged me with that humorous moniker. To this day he calls me "Guru" whenever we meet in the hall at LifeWay. Don't worry—I'm not ordering vanity plates any time soon.

The truth is, I don't feel much like a "Guru," and there is no magic formula here—no five-step program to implement, and no "money-back guarantee" for worship ministry success. It's just us—fellow servants who feel the awesome weight of leading worship in our churches and feel called to make disciples for the glory of God as we do.

This project started by imagining I was sitting across the table from a pastor who loves his church and longs for the worship ministry of his congregation to flourish and contribute to the ongoing mission. That was the burden that drove me to the keyboard to begin writing.

So grab a cup of coffee and let's begin.

Mike Harland

CHAPTER ONE

THE ESSENTIALS OF WORSHIP

Hollyhocks or squash?

That was the penetrating question around my house for several days one spring. The previous year my wife and I (mostly her) decided to raise a few squash plants in our backyard. To clear off a spot, I removed several large hollyhocks—a tall plant with large showy flowers—that to me, looked like giant weeds anyway. We planted our squash and enjoyed the fruit of our backyard experiment all summer. We were quite proud of our little garden, which also had several tomato plants.

As we were thinking about our squash plans for the next year, we noticed that something was growing back where last year's plants had been. As children of veteran gardeners, we knew that squash has to be replanted every year, but what

was growing looked like squash to us. We rational-
ized we must have left a few squash on the ground
and the seeds from them must have produced the
new plants.

Nice theory.

We were excited to think we were ahead of the
game and that we would be enjoying squash early
this year. But as the plants grew and grew and
grew, eventually becoming taller than our fence,
and then produced this beautiful little red flower,
well, we finally realized it wasn't the squash that
had come back—it was the hollyhocks.

Have you ever had fried hollyhock? Me nei-
ther. So we pulled them up and finally got the new
squash crop in the ground.

True Worship

You can't get squash from hollyhocks, and you
can't get the effects of worship from something
that isn't worship. I love to quote my dad, who told
me years ago, "Never expect someone who is not
walking with the Lord to act as though they are."

Worship—the way the Bible explains it to
us—is not just seen from the outside. It's more
than just a set of observable activities that, once

completed, equals a worship experience with the one true God.

Consider just a few examples from the Scriptures:

> Abram meets God when God speaks to him—he responds with a lifelong pursuit of obeying his Creator, all from a place of knowing God so well that the Divine calls the human his "friend." (Gen. 11)

> Joseph serves a God who reveals himself in dreams. His journey takes him from the bottom of a pit through a prison and finally to the palace of Pharaoh. (Gen. 37–50)

> Moses meets God in a bush that is burning and yet is not consumed. (Exod. 3)

> Job, through suffering, comes to a place of acknowledging, "I had heard reports about you but now my eyes have seen you. Therefore, I reject my words and am sorry for them; I am dust and ashes." (Job 42:5–6)

This worship expression of repentance comes *after* God identified Job as a righteous man.

> Saul is struck down by a blinding light on the road to Damascus and is never the same. His whole life changes direction and his pursuit becomes to "take hold of it because I also have been taken hold of by Jesus Christ." (Phil. 3:12b)

Whatever worship is, we know that it produces something in us that is visible—but not everything that is visible is worship. It is not merely the externals that characterize authenticity.

Consider the person who sings and "really means it . . ."

- the congregant that stands and lifts their hands while the choir sings
- the one who always speaks during the testimony service
- the usher, deacon, staff member, children's or student ministry volunteer, Bible study leader, all serving in the various ministries of the church
- the pastor who preaches every Sunday

- the worship "guy" trying to write a book about the essentials of worship!

All of them could be believers living out an intimate walk of worship with the Lord—or none of them could be. A nonbeliever or carnal "disciple" can imitate virtually every external activity of a believer. The key word there, of course, is "imitate."

Consider further, this person could just be singing a song they love to sing because it shows off their talent:

- Far from "not caring what anyone else thinks," this person could care so much they are willing to express something that isn't genuine just to enhance what others think of them.
- The servant endlessly working for others might not actually be putting others first, but serving to win the applause of others.
- The pastor or worship leader's ministry may be more vocational than spiritual, just because they happen to be good at it.

Authentic worship is observable in the life-change of a heart consistently moving toward alignment with God's purposes. Humility, kindness, selflessness, compassion, personal sacrifice, self-control, empathy, love for others, and a single-minded pursuit of God's kingdom expansion are just some of the visible attributes of a worshipping disciple.

Worship Wars?

Sadly, many churches today characterize their worship as "divisive" or even as a "war." It's "old versus new," "hymns versus praise songs," or even "Choir versus Praise Team." And the key word here is "versus."

Though this is common today, it certainly is not new. It often seems the twenty-first-century church leader characterizes worship controversy as something that is recent, as if we are somehow facing something never seen before.

But the divisive nature of worship is not new. Before time began, there was a worship conflict in the halls of eternity. Satan postured to attain the status of God, resulting in his expulsion. The war over who should be worshipped and how has been waged ever since.

If the purpose of our existence is to bring glory to the sovereign God, it stands to reason that Evil would purpose to deflect the praise of man away from God and to himself. This, in the most basic sense, is "spiritual warfare"—the war that Satan wages to try and keep us from worshipping God, because he hates God and because he hates us. That's why he tempted Adam and Eve in the garden, where we saw sin enter the world through man's vain attempt to become "like God." The first residents of Eden believed the lie of the serpent that they could have the worship that belonged to God, and they tasted the forbidden fruit (Gen. 3).

The early church fared no better. The apostle Paul addressed many "doubtful issues" that wreaked havoc on the early church—should we eat meat or not? What day of the week should be considered as most holy? Should women have their heads covered when they pray (Rom. 14; 1 Cor. 11)?

Christianity down through the centuries has been fighting the same fight over and over again about the musical aspects of our worship. A simple review of church history reveals concerns about the use of harmony in church music during the Renaissance period, Handel's tonality in *Messiah,* the deep reservations of hymnologists like Basil Manley in the late 1800s regarding the "new" songs, or the "7-11 songs" of contemporary worship styles.

The war goes on.

If the spiritual leaders of a church want to foster a community that reflects the biblical marks of an authentic worship culture, they will have to go beneath the externals and get to the heart of the matter—first, in themselves—and then in the church as whole.

We have to get to the *essentials* of worship.

Simple Worship

In his book *Primal,* Mark Batterson quotes Oliver Wendell Holmes: "For the simplicity on this side of complexity, I wouldn't give you a fig. But for the simplicity on the other side of complexity, for that I would give you anything I have."[1]

Basically, as Batterson explains, Holmes is calling out simplicity fueled by laziness or ignorance. "I don't know because I don't want to know." But he is also calling out our natural tendency to complicate things. Over time, we add rules and procedures to just about everything and eventually complicate things to the point of making them barely recognizable.

Additionally, Holmes seems to be expressing his admiration for simplicity on the far side of complexity. That is, a simplicity that is informed and matured by the process of becoming less complex. This is a simplicity that once was complicated, but in the search for authenticity has deliberately become simpler.

Our worship is no different.

For example—a person starts out on a faith journey. He could easily begin by wrongly assuming his worship is what endears him to God. He reads the Bible because he has to in order to stay in God's good graces. He gives, witnesses, signs up for mission trips, and sings every song because he is supposed to. He prays, but only when he needs something from a benevolent Father. Deep down, his worship becomes increasingly complex—a growing list of dos and don'ts that follow him around in his spiritual appointment book.

Then, his wife gets cancer. After the initial shock wears off, he is left with a complicated yet immature belief system. He keeps doing the same things but somehow feels betrayed by this God he is worshipping. He comes face-to-face with the fact that he doesn't know this God he praises very well.

One day, he realizes none of the things he has been doing seem to make a difference. In desperation, he goes to the Scripture in this state of mind, but no longer to put a check mark on his "To Do" list. This time, he goes in complete humility out of hunger. "God, I need to hear from you." He prays, but not the perfunctory prayers he has recited all of his life. Now, he pours out his soul to a Father who loves him. He sings, but not to hear his own voice—rather, to be heard by the only One who can step into the trial he is facing. He worships, not because anyone is watching or listening, but because his heart will explode if he doesn't open up his mouth.

As the Good Shepherd carries him through the valley of the shadow of death with his wife, his walk with God loses the complexity of religion. And with this newfound simplicity, his worship becomes real.

Some realities have to be experienced to be understood.

I knew a few things about being a father just by watching my dad. The sense of responsibility, the authority that comes with that responsibility, and the ability to make decisions for your family and children, were all things I observed about fatherhood growing up with a great dad.

But when I became a father, the whole thing changed. I knew I was supposed to take care of my children—but I had no idea how badly I would want to until the first one was born. I knew I would love them—but I didn't know I would love them more than life itself. I understood that Teresa would be my partner in parenthood—I didn't understand how the two of us would literally become one in our parenting, a bond that continues to grow till this very day.

In a similar way, understanding worship goes beyond theological exercise, though it surely is theological. It exceeds musical accomplishment, though the use of music in worship is certainly God's gift to us of an outward way of expressing our praise. It transcends any particular music style or approach, and I'm convinced the Bible demonstrates that in a very interesting way.

Think about this.

In the Psalms we are fortunate to have a number of superscriptions from the original texts that provide insightful details. A few describe the setting of the psalm, like Psalm 34 that has a superscription that reads, *"Concerning David, when he pretended to be insane in the presence of Abimelech who drove him out, and he departed."* Now we can read the psalm with a little more understanding of what it was about—like today when a song-writer explains why a song was written. People love "song stories."

The superscription of Psalm 45 intrigues me and leads me to a question. It reads, "For the choir director: according to 'The Lilies.' A Maskil of the Sons of Korah. A love song."

According to *The Lilies*? What does that mean? Well, it seems the original performance of this text was associated with a particular tune called *The Lilies*.

What in the world did that sound like? Some have given themselves to try and understand, but in the end, we really don't know.

Here's the point—if the sovereign God of the universe preserved the text of this psalm, as well as the whole Bible—and I certainly believe he did—why didn't he preserve the tune?

He could have. God could have given us the exact music to be performed. Think of all of the arguments we could have avoided if God had just handed us the appropriate music setting for worship along with the Scriptures.

After thinking about this for a decade or so, I've come to this belief: perhaps one reason God didn't preserve the tunes was so each generation could join him in creating the music. One of his divine attributes is his creativity, and since he made us in his image, we, to a lesser degree, have that same attribute. God has allowed us to express our own creative nature as we have composed the songs with him down through the ages of the church. And think about how much the music has changed. Each generation has found its own tunes and its own way of expressing his word and our worship response in song.

The tragedy would be if any particular generation came to believe they were the one that landed on the final melody. God gives every era of believers their own chance to add to the music. What a wonderful gift that is to us! We have the joy of adding our own expression to the song of faith!

When we read Revelation 15, we are struck with an amazing reality—one of the songs sung in heaven will be one that was written by one of us— Moses (Rev. 15:3)! That tells me that our Creator God has invited his creation to create music for the purpose of worship!

As we come alongside God in creating that music and creating a healthy, biblical culture of singing and worship in our churches, there are some core values we must keep in mind. The following chapters are comprised of that concise set of values that are common in churches with healthy worship cultures. The great news about a list of the essentials of a healthy, Bible-centered worship culture is that the list is very short! In other words, with God's help, *we can do this.*

And hopefully, by the time we get to the end of the book, we just might have a way to tell the difference between hollyhocks and squash.

VALUE ONE

TELL
THE STORY

CHAPTER TWO

WE NEED THE
REAL JESUS

Worship has a starting place.

In the book *Seven Words of Worship*, my coauthor Stan Moser and I use a simple definition of worship: "Worship is our only reasonable response to God's revelation."[2]

The idea is simple—worship is not something we initiate or conjure up for the purpose of convincing God to act on our behalf. It's not an exercise that dictates a reaction from a deity, nor a personal discipline intended to produce tranquility in our lives. It's not a philosophy or an approach to spirituality, nor a belief system among many belief systems attempting to bring meaning to our existence.

We worship in response to our God, who has revealed himself to us.

God has revealed himself to us and given mankind enough information about him to provoke a response of worship.

The apostle Paul writes it this way:

> For God's wrath is revealed from heaven against all godlessness and unrighteousness of people who by their unrighteousness suppress the truth, since what can be known about God is evident among them, because God has shown it to them. For his invisible attributes, that is, his eternal power and divine nature, have been clearly seen since the creation of the world, being understood through what he has made As a result, people are without excuse. (Rom. 1:18–20)

Creation alone gives us enough information to know there is a Creator. The psalmist explains this obvious truth in Psalm 24: "The earth and everything in it, the world and its inhabitants, belong to the LORD" (Ps. 24:1–2).

He goes on to ask the logical question in response to creation that has existed in the heart of humanity from the beginning: "Who may ascend the mountain of the LORD? Who may stand in his holy place?" (Ps. 24:3).

In other words, since there is a God, how can we know him? The news gets worse here, because the answer tells us that the holy character of God dictates that only the righteous can live in his presence. We're sunk at this point, because we known we are not righteous.

But the news gets better because the psalmist points to "the LORD, mighty in battle" (v. 8), who is righteous and who has won the battle for righteousness. And when we look back at Psalm 24 through the lens of the New Testament, we understand who the "LORD of Armies" (v. 10) is—it is Jesus, the one and only Son of God.

God made it all, including us, and became the Warrior who fought and won the battle for our righteousness. Our only rightful response is worship—with our lips and with our lives.

Hebrews 13:15–16 reads, "Therefore, through him let us continually offer up to God a sacrifice of praise, that is, the fruit of lips that confess his name. Don't neglect to do what is good and to share, for God is pleased with such sacrifices."

The starting place of worship is that story.

Oprah's Jesus

It was 4 o'clock in the afternoon and my day at the offices of LifeWay Worship was winding down. I convinced myself to go across the street and work out at the YMCA before heading home. After I changed into my running clothes and found an empty treadmill in the workout area, I started stretching and finally hit the "quick start" button on the machine. Just when I was at full speed, I noticed the program on the TV screen at the far wall of the room. It was Oprah.

Now I've never watched much of her program and immediately wondered how I could change the channel when suddenly the subject of her show caught my attention. Oprah, along with a panel of experts that included two ministers from Christian denominations, were talking about Jesus. Now she had my attention. I increased the speed to 4.5.

To this point I had no idea what Oprah might have thought about Jesus. I was aware that she professed a "spiritual" sense of being and that quite often she would address those beliefs. She is on record for criticizing the faith she was raised up to believe—a faith that proclaimed Jesus as the Son of God he claimed to be. Her testimony is that one day, she realized all she had been taught was wrong, and so she began a search that resulted in finding "God" within herself. A quick "YouTube" search will quickly satisfy any curiosity about what she says she believes—interesting to say the least.

As the panel continued, several fascinating observations were made by the guests—that Jesus was in fact real and at one time walked the earth, that he was a kind man and said many great things, that if anyone wanted to make him the center of their spirituality and that worked for them, that was okay. The panel, seemingly more interested in what Oprah thought than what Jesus thought, went along with all this as if it was perfectly acceptable to God for everyone to have their own equally legitimate opinion about Jesus.

While I watched this, I got so worked up that before I knew it I was mumbling back to the screen and running faster and faster on the treadmill! The consensus of Oprah and the panel seemed to be, "I like the Jesus that I believe in. I just don't like the one the Bible talks about." The more they discussed it, the closer I came to almost flying off that treadmill.

I couldn't help it anymore. In total frustration, I said out loud back to the screen, "The problem with your Jesus is that your Jesus isn't the One coming back!" Then I looked around to see if anyone was listening to me! I thought it odd that here I was at the Young Men's Christian Association— an organization that bears his name—watching a program that said all this about Jesus. It was rather disturbing.

My mind went immediately to Acts 1:11 and the statement the angels made to the disciples on the hillside right after Jesus had ascended to heaven: "Men of Galilee, why do you stand looking up into heaven? *This same Jesus,* who has been taken from you into heaven, will come in the same way that you have seen him going into heaven" (emphasis mine).

This same Jesus. This *very* Jesus. I wanted so badly to warn Oprah and her guests that the Jesus coming back is the One that left—not the one they had created. And the One that left is the King of kings and Lord of lords, and at his name, every knee—theirs and the rest of the world's—will one day bow. The opinions of her panel, or anyone else, won't matter then.

Your Own Personal Jesus?

This illustrates a huge problem across the world today—everyone has their own Jesus.

Many people caught in a post-modern ideology don't know who Jesus really is. In the enlightened thinking of our day, there is plenty of room for everyone's Jesus—he can be a good man, a teacher, a son of God among many sons of God, a brother to Muhammad, a cousin to Buddha (I made up that one), or whoever you want or need him to be. He can be gay, married, and whatever else suits you. Sadly, churches can accommodate this mind-set by losing their focus on the real Jesus.

The problem with any "Jesus" that we create is that, by virtue of the fact we created him, our "Jesus" has no right to rule our lives. Rather than being created in his image, we create him in ours. As a matter of fact, as his creator, he exists only to accommodate our own desires. You've seen the "Build-a-Bear" stores in the mall, haven't you? Well, in today's mind-set, we have a "Build-a-Jesus" mentality, and we make him into whatever our lifestyle and preferences need him to be. The whole thing is upside down.

Churches with healthy worship cultures have a clear and biblical view of Jesus. Their hunger for truth and their desire to know the Word of God has given them a clear view of who Jesus really is—the Holy Son of God, the Way, the Truth, and the Life (John 14:6). All of Scripture points to the deity of Jesus Christ. His person and presence rests on every page.

In Colossians 3:16, Paul writes a powerful statement about worship, "Let the word of Christ dwell richly among you, in all wisdom teaching and admonishing one another through psalms, hymns, and spiritual songs, singing to God with gratitude in your hearts."

Followers of Christ learn the truth about Jesus through the songs we sing together. We actually teach and encourage each other as we sing songs about him.

We tend to focus on the "how" of that verse and spend our energies on what "psalms, hymns, and spiritual songs" actually means. But I'm convinced the real starting place of worship is in the first phrase: "Let the word of Christ dwell richly among you." In other words, let the Word of God that contains the truth about Jesus pulsate at the core of your being. And I'm convinced Paul was, at least in part, referring back to the powerful song about Jesus he had written just two chapters before in Colossians 1:15–20:

He is the image of the invisible God, the firstborn over all creation. For everything was created by him, in heaven and on earth, the visible and the invisible, whether thrones or dominions or rulers or authorities— all things, have been created through him and for him. He is before all things, and by him all things hold together. He is also the head of the body, the church; he is the begin- ning, the firstborn from the dead, so that he might come to have first place in everything. For God was pleased to have all his fullness dwell in him, and through him to recon- cile everything to himself, whether things on earth or things in heaven, by making peace through his blood, shed on the cross.

Seeing Jesus

Several years ago I was asked to lead worship at the New Mexico Baptist Convention Evangelism Conference at Hoffmantown Baptist Church in Albuquerque. There were several things about this assignment that made it special for me. First, my close friend and gifted Bible teacher Wayne Barber was pastor there at the time, and I knew I'd get to spend some time with him. Also, my friend and mentor Jim Shaddix was speaking at the conference, and to top it off, one of my partners in ministry and cowriter of many songs, Luke Garrett, was there as well. The other part I was so excited about was that I would be working with Anne Graham Lotz, leading worship before she spoke twice during the conference. I knew I was in for a special time!

I had read several of Anne's books through the years and heard her speak on television and radio several times. I've always been blessed by the profound teaching gift God has given to Anne and intrigued by the experiences of the daughter of the great evangelist, Billy Graham.

But I wasn't ready for this.

Anne really only has one message. In every conference and every conversation, one recurring truth permeates her words. As I listened, that message was coming through to me loud and clear. Then, in the evening session, Anne spoke from her book *I Saw the Lord*. This message centers on Isaiah's vision outlined in Isaiah 6. She went on to describe her own experience of "seeing the

Lord, high and lifted up" and the life change that brought to her. When she finished speaking, she wrote something in the front of the copy of her book she read from that night and before I knew it, her assistant had pressed it into my hand. I opened the cover to find a message for me from Anne, thanking me for my partnership in the ministry of the conference.

Several days later, I was in my home study and I took out the book she had given me. My wife had read her own copy of the book several years before, and I remember reading parts of it as well. But that morning I dug into the central truth of Anne's life and of that book. The only way to know God is to see—to really know and experience—the person of Jesus Christ.

And though I had been a Christian for many years, on that day—for the first time in a long time—*I wanted to see Jesus.*

I remember asking the Lord to give me a right view of who he really is—to show me what Isaiah saw and what Anne was talking about. It wasn't long before I found myself on my knees, crying out to him for his forgiveness, for his fresh mercy and grace in my life. I stayed there for hours, eventually calling my assistant and asking her to clear my day. I could barely walk out of the room.

It was my own miniature version of Isaiah 6. To be sure, nothing I experienced that day was a result of my spirituality. I am ashamed to say that sin I had never thought about before came right to the surface that morning. I'm equally ashamed to say that even now, my own flesh often keeps me from walking in full view of Christ every day. But this much I learned that day: only when I have a right view of who Jesus is—his holiness, his righteousness, his glory, his love—can I walk in the power of his Spirit, and see myself and the world around me the way he does. Then and only then can I truly worship "in Spirit and in truth," as described in John 4:24.

In Isaiah 6 we see the marks that accompany a genuine vision of who Jesus is—conviction that comes over us, confession that comes out of us, cleansing that comes in us, and a commission that comes to us. I wonder sometimes, in this era when worship is so emphasized in so many of our churches, why we don't see more of these evidences in our churches?

Could it be that we are seeing more expression, more music, more energy, more talent, more technology, more strategy, more skill, and more of everything else you can think of—but less Jesus?

As Anne Graham Lotz says in *I Saw the Lord*, "One of the lasting impacts of personal revival is that it has made a difference in my life. I not only listen to the voice of Jesus and apply His words to my life, but I live for Him alone. I am so caught up in who He is and what He has done for me that I no longer consider my life my own. My life is laid down at His nail-pierced feet, totally available for His use. Anytime. Anywhere. Anyway. The supreme joy of my life is to be available to Him."[3]

Does your "Jesus" require that of you? If he doesn't, then your Jesus is no different than Oprah's.

None of us will ever forget the vicious attack on our nation in September of 2001. But I'm afraid most of us missed the attack that had an even more devastating effect on the spiritual condition of our culture than the planes that flew into the World Trade Center and the Pentagon on September 11. The attack I'm talking about happened at Yankee Stadium on September 23, just twelve days after the terrorists crashed those planes. It was titled "Prayer for America" and was organized and hosted by Oprah Winfrey.

The service included leaders from every imaginable faith—Christian, Islam, Buddhist, even New Age and Agnostic—all there to pray to the

"God" of their understanding, or should I say, misunderstanding. Every speaker seemed to be saying in one way or another, "We all really do worship the same God, no matter what we call her or him."[4]

One observer identified what they thought was the absolute highlight of the service—Bette Midler singing that classic song of prayer (tongue firmly planted in cheek), "Wind Beneath My Wings."

This service was an all-out attack on truth—a re-characterization of who God is for all of America. Instead of planes flying into buildings, we had human lies being flown into the time-less tower of God's truth and setting the souls of humanity on fire. The biggest difference is that God's truth has not and will not collapse under their attack.

The "Coexist" ideology is this same sentimental gobbledygook that brought us my least favorite bumper sticker—the one that has every religious symbol known to man, implying that they are all equal and we can all worship God "no matter what we call her or him." There's only one problem with that noble idea—it's a lie.

What would have happened if on that day the crowd that filled Yankee Stadium had cried out to the One and Only True Living God, Jesus

Christ himself? What if we had laid aside all the "political correctness" that had to accommodate everyone's view, and simply bowed in humble acknowledgment that God is God, and that we needed him to intervene in our chaos? What if we had confessed our sin and rose to declare to our enemies and the world, "Our God is in heaven, and does whatever he pleases" (Ps. 115:3). What if we had taken the opportunity to respond to the attacks on our nation by calling the Islamic world into a right understanding of the person and nature of our triune God, and declared to them that Jesus was willing and ready to forgive their sin and bring peace to their souls? What if?

This is not a new problem though.

In his biography of the great theologian Dietrich Bonhoeffer, Eric Metaxas recounts Bonhoeffer's own journal during his year-long visit to New York in 1930–31. In one entry Bonhoeffer writes, "In New York they preach about virtually everything; only one thing is not addressed, or is addressed so rarely that I have as yet been unable to hear it, namely, the gospel of Jesus Christ, the cross, sin and forgiveness, death, and life."[5]

Bonhoeffer was so disenchanted with the preaching he heard as a seminary student at prestigious Union Seminary in New York and during his many visits to the Protestant churches of New York at the time, he looked elsewhere for the gospel, eventually associating with a large African-American church where the truth about Jesus was preached with conviction. Perhaps the absence of those seeds of truth in that era found their logical result in the all-out assault on the truth at Yankee Stadium in 2001.

The Bible is clear—when all of the universe finally sees and acknowledges who Jesus is, every knee will bow. The only people who don't worship him now are those who haven't seen who he is to this point. On the day they do, they will go to their knees.

Churches that understand worship understand the truth of who Jesus is—the only begotten son of God, perfect in every way; the One who laid down his life to pay for our sin. He is not *a* way to God, he is *the* way to God, because Jesus *is* God. Jesus didn't go to the cross to give us a nice option. He went because it was the only option. He wasn't "Plan B." Jesus was—and is—the eternal plan. That's not intolerance—it's the truth.

Churches with healthy worship cultures start right there—with a clear vision of Jesus and songs that teach about him and admonish the church with his Word.

CHAPTER THREE

TELLING THE STORY

I come from a long line of storytellers.

Whenever the Harland family gathers and usually after we have enjoyed an enormous meal prepared by my mom, the stories of our childhood start to roll. My sister, brother, and I are the central figures in the stories that have been shared so often, the in-laws and grandchildren are starting to think they lived through them too. We share stories about ballgames and mission trips, moves to new towns, and family events that can fill an entire evening at my parents' house. Laughter fills the packed-out room.

If we all are together for more than a few hours, there is one particular story that will be retold, at least in some form, before we all go home. It's the one about our family vacation to Kentucky.

It was mid-August in 1969, and our family was going camping in a state park outside Bowling

Green. Throughout my youth, our family vacations were usually in a campground of one type or another. It wasn't until we were all grown that I learned my mother really didn't enjoy camping that much, but since it was the most cost-effective way for our family of five to enjoy an adventure together, my dad packed up the Sears tent and Coleman stove and headed for a campground somewhere within driving distance of Corinth, Mississippi—this time, it was Bowling Green.

There was something else that happened in August of 1969 that is central to this story. One of the largest and most destructive hurricanes to ever make landfall in the United States hit the Gulf Coast of Mississippi—Hurricane Camille. You might think, *How did that affect your vacation in Bowling Green, Kentucky?*

If you were alive then, you may recall that one of the reasons Camille was so devastating was that it remained strong for many hundreds of miles after it hit land and eventually made its way all the way to . . . you guessed it . . . Bowling Green, Kentucky. Just as we finished setting up our tent, a deluge flooded our tent and us. The night before, my dad had lost his wallet at a carnival, and now all of our clothes were ruined and mud was everywhere. Undaunted, the mighty Harland vacation went right on. We stayed right there in that mess for the whole week.

As the story goes, after several days, we finally decided it was time to leave. With $5 and a gas credit card, we set out for home, stopping off in Nashville for a bucket of chicken and a free tour of the Parthenon. We must have looked like the Beverly Hillbillies going through that art exhibit that day!

That story in many ways characterizes the Harland family and illustrates how important stories are to any family. My mom has a saying I have heard all of my life: "Nothing is a problem unless you make it a problem." That vacation is her "proof-text" for that axiom. Our family was truly making "lemonade out of lemons" that week in Bowling Green. To this day, the story brings laughter and joy every time we tell it.

Stories and Songs

The children of God have many stories to tell, and each church has its own story that characterizes God's work among that congregation through the years. As a member of Brentwood Baptist Church, I love to hear my pastor, Dr. Mike Glenn, tell the story of how years ago a small group of laypeople meeting in the basement of the Tennessee Baptist Children's Home passed around a yellow legal pad and signed up for their own portion of the debt to finance the church's first building. That legal pad was taken to a nearby bank, and the construction project was funded. It encourages me every time I think about that moment in our church's history and the faith of those charter members.

Ministries that understand the link between testimony and worship will always find room for the stories of their people. A beautiful example of this can be found in Psalm 107.

It begins, "Give thanks to the LORD, for he is good; his faithful love endures forever" (Ps. 107:1). Then, over the course of the psalm, four different stories emerge of people that cried out to God in their distress: the lost (vv. 4–9), the imprisoned (vv. 10–16), the foolish (vv. 11–22), and those overwhelmed by a storm (vv. 23–32). In every case, they "cried out to the LORD in their trouble," and God heard and delivered them. When they were rescued, each one gave "thanks to the LORD for his faithful love" (vv. 8, 15, 21, 31). The psalm closes with the testimony shared by them all: "But he lifts the needy out of their suffering" (v. 41). Psalm 107 beautifully illustrates the testimony of praise that flows out of hearts that have been set free.

Sharing our stories—the testimonies of God's grace in our lives, the experiences of his faithfulness, and the foundational truths of his Word we have seen at work in our daily living—is an important attribute of a healthy worshipping culture.

In his letter to the Ephesians, Paul is teaching a vital message to the church. He calls for unity and patience from all as each one works out their faith using their different gifts for the benefit of all. He compels his brothers and sisters to walk in love for each other and to consistently display an attitude of mutual submission.

Right in the middle of the letter, he instructs the church to "be filled by the Spirit: speaking to one another in psalms, hymns, and spiritual songs, singing and making music in your heart to the Lord" (Eph. 5:18–19).

Theologians have debated the nuances of the different meanings of the three types of expressions found in this verse—psalms, hymns, and spiritual songs. I have nothing to offer here that adds to that discussion, but I do understand the meaning of "speaking," and I'm fairly confident I understand, "singing and making music in your heart to the Lord."

With certainty, we can derive from this text that there are multiple ways to give utterance to the story, and we should use them all for that purpose. The community of faith is a testifying community for the benefit of everyone in it. Believers encourage and exhort each other with the testimonies we share with each other.

We do that with singing, but we also do that by speaking to one another. As a matter of fact, taken literally, the text seems to say that the "music" happens in the heart of the singer. There's nothing here that says others hear it.

All of this is contingent on a pretext: "being filled with the Spirit." In other words, in communities of faith, where the people are Spirit-filled, there will be speech and song that is shared openly with each other. Somewhere along the way, we have seemed to accept that singing is for singers, but the Bible clearly says that believers will testify to each other from hearts that are filled with music.

Healthy worship cultures know this reality. The church doesn't gather to watch something or to hear something. It gathers to "do something." And that "something" is telling their stories of faith for the benefit of all.

Nik Ripken described his own discovery of this principle in his book *The Insanity of God*. In the wake of a crisis of belief after experiencing personal tragedy and difficulty in his mission journey, Nik interviewed hundreds of persecuted believers around the world trying to identify how faith can flourish in the face of intense pressure. From those interviews Nik was able to see patterns of faith in practice that were common to believers from the persecuted church in the Far East, Middle East, Asia, and beyond.

Throughout the book, Nik recounts stories of how the song born through adversity flows out of the heart of believers and is shared with each other. He writes: "When I finally connected enough of the dots, I came to understand the significance of music as a faith factor and recognize its presence and power already at work in the Islamic world."

He continues: "I have always believed that Jesus was serious about his final earthly instructions to his followers. I have always believed that he indeed wants us to reach the world with his message."[6]

The "heartsong," as he describes it, is born in the heart of the believer walking in faith no matter what hardship may come. When the song is sung then, it declares the gospel with a power the enemy cannot withstand.

Nik recounts the story of one such song that a brother in prison sang every day, much to the dismay of his captors. The beatings and punishment he would endure for singing the song could not stop the prisoner from singing it, day after day.

Finally, as he was led to his apparent execution, the entire population of the prison sang the song together as he took the final march. The guards were so stunned by the singing they released their hold on him and eventually released him altogether. They could not silence the song and they couldn't stand to hear it, so they released the prisoner.

Throughout the book, Nik recounts conversation after conversation with believers who suffered brutal persecution for their faith. In the concluding pages of the chapter titled "Heartsongs," he concludes, "I was beginning to wonder if it was time for me to start to sing again."[7]

But our story isn't the most important one we tell.

We tell the story of God's faithfulness every time we lift our song of worship, whether we are in a prison or a pew. God's deliverance of his people puts a song in our hearts that cannot be contained.

The "heartsongs" of the church from across the world all come together to create a single story that encompasses them all. Our stories all come out of one story—the story of Jesus, the Lamb of God, who takes away the sin of the world. Healthy worship ministries lead the church in singing the story of the scarlet thread that permeates Scripture.

The long-time pastor of First Baptist Church, Dallas, Dr. W. A. Criswell, was known for a particular message he preached throughout his life. He first preached it on New Year's Eve 1961 in the pulpit of First Baptist. Spanning from Genesis to Revelation, Dr. Criswell expounded for several hours the gospel thread of redemption that runs throughout the narrative of the entire Bible. For the rest of his life, he continued to add to this message that has been modified and shared by many others to this very day, years after his death.

Take a moment and think about the songs that are sung in your church week after week. Imagine that someone started attending your church that had never read the Bible, never heard a sermon, and had never heard the name of Jesus in his or her life. Further suppose that for the few weeks that person attended they only heard the songs you sang—no sermon, no testimony, and no other information.

How much of the story would they hear in the songs you sing?

In his book *The Worship Pastor*, Zac Hicks explores the variety of roles the worship pastor assumes while leading the worship ministry of a church. One example is the role of curator. He says, "A worship pastor keeps in mind the biblical role in aiding the church's experience of the presence of God."[8]

With that in mind, the worship leader is sensitive to the musical sensibilities of the congregation and constantly aware of the types of "sung prayer" represented in the songs we sing—"praise, adoration, thanksgiving, confession, petition, intercession, and supplication." He goes further to say that the leader must recognize how the music "forms a church's ecclesiology."[9]

For many years, churches have sung hymns that declare the whole gospel. These lyrics continue to resonate with believers across the centuries. To illustrate this, let's look at one such lyric written in the late nineteenth century by J. Wilber Chapman.

> *One day when Heaven was filled with*
> *His praises,*
> *One day when sin was as black as*
> *could be,*

Jesus came forth to be born of a virgin,
Dwelt among men, my example is He!

Refrain:
Living, He loved me; dying, He saved
    me;
Buried, He carried my sins far away;
Rising, He justified freely forever;
One day He's coming—oh, glorious
    day!

One day they led Him up Calvary's
    mountain,
One day they nailed Him to die on the
    tree;
Suffering anguish, despised and
    rejected:
Bearing our sins, my Redeemer is He!

One day they left Him alone in the
    garden,
One day He rested, from suffering free;
Angels came down o'er His tomb to
    keep vigil;
Hope of the hopeless, my Savior is He!

One day the grave could conceal Him
    no longer,

*One day the stone rolled away from
the door;
Then He arose, over death He had
conquered;
Now is ascended, my Lord evermore!*

*One day the trumpet will sound for
His coming,
One day the skies with His glories will
shine;
Wonderful day, my beloved ones
bringing;
Glorious Savior, this Jesus is mine!*
(public domain)

This powerful lyric tells the whole story of Jesus! It begins with his birth, tells of his death, burial, and resurrection, and proclaims his promised return to claim his bride, the church. Charles Marsh wrote the classic tune associated with this hymn, and Christians have sung it for many years.

Contemporary songwriters Michael Bleeker and Mark Hall composed a modern setting for this lyric in 2009 titled "Glorious Day" that was recorded by the group Casting Crowns. Their version introduced it to a whole new generation of believers who are singing the story of Jesus every time they sing it.

Modern hymn writers are also telling the story with clarity. Stuart Townend and Keith Getty have coauthored "In Christ Alone" and "Oh, to See the Dawn (The Power of the Cross)"—two powerful settings of the gospel story sung by disciples all over the world. Whenever the church sings these accurate and biblical descriptions of the atoning work of Christ, they are declaring the story for all to hear and understand.[10]

In the great hymns of our history and in the modern songs of today we see the church telling the story of redemption in song. As we will see in the later chapters, the theology of hymns and songs like these have an amazing impact on the souls of those who sing them. Healthy worship ministries understand this fact.

To be clear, hymns and songs that express emotion have an important place in our worship as well. But a warning is needed here: ministries that only include songs of emotional expression can lead to services that foster "emotionalism." Emotion in worship is good; emotionalism can actually hinder worship.

Healthy worship ministries give testimony to the stories of God's grace at work in his people, and to *the* story of grace revealed in the redemptive work of Jesus Christ. And the consistent telling of those stories can shape the worship culture of each community of faith. All of our stories begin and end with one story that we must tell—and sing—over and over again.

In 2015, the Christian band Big Daddy Weave released a song, "My Story," that beautifully captures this healthy attribute of worship. The chorus ends with, "For to tell you my story is to tell of him."[11]

Our story. His story.

Sing it, Church.

VALUE TWO

MAKE TRUE DISCIPLES

CHAPTER FOUR

MELODY AND TRUTH

Music can be dangerous.

Those of us who teach and preach with the language of music had better be respectful of its great power. It is not to be used for manipulation or self-promotion, though music is composed of properties that can easily do both.

Think about your favorite movie scenes and reflect on what the music does to draw out emotion. If you read those scripts, they likely wouldn't move you very much. You could even observe the scene, but if you took the soundtrack away it would fall flat and emotionless. The giant shark in *Jaws* wouldn't scare us nearly as much without the two-note underscore that builds in intensity throughout the movie.

It was Plato who said, "Music is a moral law. It gives soul to the universe, wings to the mind, flight to the imagination, and charm and gaiety to life." As Christ-followers, Plato's attribution to music makes us a little nervous—after all, everything he says about music is rightly attributable to our God. The point is not lost that music itself can be a god to anyone who wishes to worship it.

Consider Nebuchadnezzar, the mighty emperor of Babylon. In Daniel 3 we read the story of the king building a statue of himself and then commanding everyone to bow down and worship him. He knew that a soundtrack would enhance the spirit of the people. So he called together all the musicians—the horn, flute, pipe, lyre, harp, and drum specifically mentioned—and then the phrase, "every kind of music," for the purpose of playing the very first "Stand Up" chord that would kick off the worship of the pagan king.

A couple of years ago a newly discovered artist performed on the televised Country Music Awards. His performance was the one everyone was talking about the next day. It was a duet with an established star. When I watched a clip of it later, I had to admit, the performance was amazing. People were swaying and raising their hands—responding audibly and visibly to the music as if they were in church—and the song was about drinking whiskey.

Music can move human emotion like few other mediums of art. But music can also inform the intellect in amazing ways. Parents know this intuitively—we teach our children the alphabet with a melody. My grown-up daughter can still sing the fifty states in alphabetical order because of a song she learned in the sixth grade. I've heard melodies that help people memorize the books of the Bible, the presidents of our country, Scripture memory, and a list of the fruit of the Spirit.

Neuroscience continues to discover the powerful link between music and the human brain. Videos of individuals suffering from memory disease singing songs of their youth without missing a word have gone viral across the Internet. My first experience singing in a memory care facility brought this to light for me years ago. I started the first hymn with, "What can wash away my sin?" and then was stunned in amazement when people who could not remember their own names sang in reply, "Nothing but the blood of Jesus." Then, for the next thirty minutes, I led them in singing hymns and quickly realized they remembered more of the words than I did.

My oldest son Lee is completing his PhD dissertation in musicology at the time of this writing. His research focuses on the middle symphonies of a greatly respected composer at the turn of the twentieth century, Gustav Mahler. In this research, Lee is identifying an observable link between the theoretical structure of the compositions and the worldview of the composer. In other words, the music Mahler was creating had a direct link to his belief system at the time. His music had meaning.

In this research, Lee is pointing to something that Nebuchadnezzar apparently knew: that music, one of God's great gifts to us, has intrinsic qualities that impact human emotion and intellect in profound ways. Consider every great movement in human history, both for good and evil. Virtually all of them had a musical component accompanying the movement.

Consider the Reformation and "A Mighty Fortress Is Our God," the abolition of slavery and "Amazing Grace," the Civil Rights movement and "We Shall Overcome." There are many, many more examples.

"Revive Us Again"

Singing marked the spiritual revivals and awakenings in church history. In the book *Sing!*, Keith and Kristyn Getty explain, "Since the dawn of the church, times of great church renewal and revival have been accompanied by (and, we might say, spurred on by) churches singing. . . . Luther and the Reformers inspired and enabled their congregations to sing together in their own language, in words that they and the people around them could understand. It was revolutionary."[12] If we hope for the Lord to revive us again, we ought to be doing all we can to create healthy worship cultures in our churches that proclaim truth and point to the glory of God.

Churches with healthy worship ministries proclaim truth.

We know music has power to affect people. Consequently, when you combine the qualities of music with the "two-edged sword" of Scripture, you have a mighty tool of impact in the hands of the servants of God.

Psalm 149:6 reads, "Let the exultation of God be in their mouths and a double-edged sword in their hands." In context, this is describing the new song of praise infused with power of the Word of God.

The psalm goes on to describe what this weapon does: ". . . inflicting vengeance on the nations and punishment on the peoples, binding their kings with chains and their dignitaries with iron shackles, carrying out the judgment decreed against them" (Ps. 149:7–9a).

In other words, the truth of God's Word, carried by the music of God's people, brings God's justice to the world! I wonder how many people in our churches understand that our singing is one of the ways God brings his righteousness into the human condition—that our voices wage war in the spiritual realm, leading sinners to repent and receive the righteousness of Christ?

The psalm concludes with this acknowledgment: "This honor is for all his faithful people. Hallelujah!" (Ps. 149:9b). It is an honor for God's people to carry his truth in song to the world.

What Is that in Your Hand?

In Exodus 4, God calls Moses into action with a simple question. Verse 2 says, "What is that in your hand?" Obviously, God could see what Moses had in his hand but in this moment, God wanted Moses to see what God can do with when he has control of our simple possessions. Moses responds, "A staff." And, from there God demonstrates to Moses just what God can do with the small resources of humanity.

Matthew 14 is another story of God's desire to take what we have and do the miraculous for the benefit of many. A little boy brings Jesus two fish and five loaves and with it, Jesus feeds thousands of people, including the little boy.

Worship leaders have the amazing opportunity to give over to God the amazing tool of music that we have in our hands. We know of its power. But, have we seen what God can do with it when we yield it to him? It is a tragedy when we use this powerful resource for ourselves and fail to surrender it to God for benefit of his people.

In 2018, our nation was shocked by a tragic school shooting in Florida. A troubled young man walked into a school and wreaked havoc on the student body, tragically ending the life of seventeen students. As information about the event began to disseminate, we learned that armed and trained officers were at the school in time to intervene but failed to act in time. They only talked back and forth to each other while the gunman executed those high school students!

To be fair to those officers, I don't know how I would respond in a moment like that—but I would hope if I were called to act, I would respond to that calling with action!

In the spiritual realm, we are soldiers in a battle, "equipped for every good work" (2 Tim. 3:17). And we are called to engage. But how many soldiers stand by as we sing, even though this weapon has been placed in our hands?

Churches with healthy worship ministries have leaders that understand it matters greatly what they sing.

I once had a friend who bought an expensive car known for its extreme acceleration and speed. He picked me up to go for a ride with him and totally stunned me when he drove to a remote highway outside the city and took the car up to speeds beyond 150 mph! I was terrified!

Then he asked me if I wanted to drive. I didn't really want to, but his prodding put me behind the wheel, and before I knew it, I was driving. To say I had respect for what this machine could do would be putting it mildly. I might have nudged 100 mph but was very aware the entire time how quickly this thing could get away from me!

Just as I had to have a great deal of respect for the power of that car, worship leaders should have a great deal of respect for the power of music to influence what people feel, and even more importantly, what they believe. This is not a weapon to be wielded lightly, but a God-given, Spirit-empowered tool to be used with prayer and precision.

Healthy worship leaders curate songs for content, not just style.

If someone attended your church, but only came to the music portion of the corporate worship time and derived all of their belief system from the theological content of the songs, what would they believe? How much information about Jesus would they know? How about the Trinity? The doctrine of grace? What it means to trust in Christ or to walk in faith? Or would the music of your church only communicate to them what they should feel?

The "liturgy" of a healthy church has a sense of "systematic theology."

A *systematic theology* can be defined this way: a form of theology in which the aim is to arrange spiritual truths in a self-consistent whole. Not only do healthy worship leaders curate for content in each song, they aim to present a "whole" approach of theology in song. These ministries don't just pick a few attributes of God to sing about, they aspire to cover as much of God's character and instruction as possible.

Consider the variety of psalms found in Scripture:

- Lament (community and individual)
- Imprecatory
- Penitential
- Thanksgiving (communal and individual)
- Hymn and Doxology
- Covenant Psalms
- Praise/Enthronement
- Songs of Zion
- Liturgical
- Wisdom Psalms
- Poems

And this is a simple and in no way exhaustive list. The variety of most churches pales in comparison to the variety of the psalms. The healthy worship ministry aspires for more than just a few types of songs.

Healthy worship ministries have a set of production values with intentional purpose.

Because these churches understand the gravity of this responsibility, they make choices around technical support in sound and lighting that reflect this understanding. They aspire to make sure nothing distracts from the music and truth. We explore this further in chapter 9.

Healthy worship ministries organize for maximum impact.

Effective worship ministries understand that the layers of the ministry organization can be designed to have even more impact through music. These ministries do more than prepare music for Sunday morning—they infuse into the lives of their people resources and opportunities for development through worship. Instead of involving a few musically talented people in the leadership of this ministry, they build teams of volunteers and participants that can be developed and influenced through music and truth.

I've observed something many times through the years—the number of pastors and church leaders whose first experiences of service came through a music ministry of the church they attended as a child or student is staggering. Healthy worship ministries understand the opportunities this ministry can present to develop disciples in their own faith journey and try to use those opportunities for as many people as possible—not just for the few exceptional musicians.

Coda

Balto is one of the most famous dogs in history. In 1925, the Siberian husky led a team of dogs carrying a life-saving antidote to Nome, a remote village in Alaska that had been ravaged by diphtheria. He was trained to be a winning sled dog, but when it counted the most, his training equipped this dog to brave horrible conditions and deliver a serum that saved many lives. Stories and books have been written about this remarkable animal. A statue of Balto was placed in Central Park in New York, and an animated Disney film told the story to millions.

Musicians in biblical worship cultures know what's at stake. The tool we have been given is powerful. We could use it to pursue artistic accomplishment—winning sled races. Or we could use it to proclaim truth—delivering the life-saving serum to a devastated world.

Disciples who know the language of music have a great responsibility to understand the power of this tool and to use it for the making of disciples. They may have been trained to perform, but they understand their training has a higher purpose. They may have the ability to create, but the purpose for their creativity goes beyond artistic accomplishment.

In the same way, disciple-making musicians understand the importance of mastering their craft. In many ways, music works just like a language. Imagine someone who feels called by God to serve in a foreign mission setting. For months or even years, they will study the culture and learn the language. They do this at great cost and with complete focus because they understand that even though they know the message thoroughly, they will be ineffective sharing the gospel if they don't understand the context of their culture and gain a mastery of their language.

Since God has given us a weapon that declares his justice, stirs our emotions, and stimulates our intellect, healthy worship ministries utilize their opportunities using this tool to develop disciples and advance the kingdom of God. The healthy worshipping church has disciples who are engaged in God's mission using music and truth—the irresistible weapon of praise.

We need to consider the awesome medium God gave us in music and determine to steward it with the truth of God's Word remaining the focal point. If we aren't very careful, we can love what we do for the sake of the music. Healthy worship ministries know we need to love Jesus more, and serve him with the amazing instrument of melody and truth that he has placed in our hands.

CHAPTER FIVE

MAKING TRUE DISCIPLES

I don't remember the first time this thought crossed my mind, but somewhere along the way, I realized something significant about leading music in a church that changed the way I thought about my work. This realization still impacts me.

We are not called to make music—we are called to make disciples.

If my life was all about creating music, I'd be perfectly happy for artistry and musicianship to shape my goals. My days would be filled with music and the making of it. My relationships would all be dedicated to the pursuit of some artistic accomplishment. And on a human level, honestly, I'd love it—music is just that special to me. And therein lies the danger for church musicians.

The making of music can be a very mean-ingful and rich pursuit with or without anyone else. It can completely consume the artist to the point that meaningful relationships outside of the music world can be difficult to cultivate. Ever try to have a conversation with a guitar player while he's playing?

In the church setting, musicians can easily become isolated from others in the church. They rehearse when no one else is around and often operate independently of other staff. They hang out together, and even speak, to some degree, their own language.

In larger facilities, the musician's office is often located near the rehearsal space, away from the pastor and other ministers. After all, the only thing a musician is doing is listening to music, right?

At the same time, some pastors only think of music as the part of the service that happens before they preach. I've actually had pastors say to me things like, "Just give me thirty minutes to preach. Beyond that, there's not really anything else I need you to do."

Somewhere a little further down the road, another thought came to me: *Music in and of itself is not a message to proclaim—it is a language to carry the gospel.*

Healthy worship cultures understand the role music has in discipleship and orchestrate their ministry to fulfill that mission. In these ministries, every decision regarding worship—from song choice to stage décor—is affected by the realization that music is a strategic part of the mission. The person shepherding this ministry has the great opportunity to frame the narrative around that mission and away from tedious subjects like the balance of hymns and worship songs, or praise teams versus choirs. Ministries that focus on the right things have fewer conflicts over the specific choice of music approaches and more celebrations for the outcomes of the ministry.

Leaders are wise to identify just what they are aiming for as they execute their strategy. If they are aiming at music balance—whether through multiple services of varying styles or a blended approach in the same service—they may or may not be contributing to the overall mission of the church, even if they're hitting the target they've set for themselves.

Looking at the Right Scoreboard

It was 2009. The Texas Longhorns were playing Nebraska in the Big 12 football championship game. Texas, with their standout QB, Colt McCoy, was the overwhelming favorite to win, but somehow late in the game, Nebraska was leading Texas 12–10. The Longhorns had the ball and had moved into field goal range with eight seconds to go.

Out of time-outs, Colt McCoy took the snap and started rolling to his right as the clock was winding down. Inexplicably, he seemed to be wasting time as the clock got closer and closer to zero. You could imagine every Longhorn fan in the world screaming at the TV, "Throw it away! Throw it away!" He finally did, and only a replay allowed one second to be put back on the clock so Texas could win the game, 13–12, on a last-second field goal.

Later, when asked why he waited so long to stop the clock by throwing the ball away, McCoy explained, "I was looking at the wrong clock at the snap. For a couple of seconds I was looking at the play clock instead of the game clock."

Healthy churches don't repeat that mistake.

Churches that make decisions intended to "keep the peace" or placate a segment of the congregation are looking at the wrong score-board. You will never achieve unity by eliminating conflict because you will never chase down all the issues—new ones will emerge every day.

There has to be a higher purpose. And there is.

Concentric Circles of Discipleship

So how does that work and what does that look like in a healthy worship ministry? It works in four concentric circles.

The first and smallest circle for worship leaders represents *self and those closest to us.* We make disciples through worship first by being a worshipping disciple ourselves through Bible study, private and corporate worship, and leadership in the home with our families. Then, we pour our best energy into engaging in worship with those closest to us.

The second and somewhat bigger circle represents the *people we serve with in worship ministry*—members of the choir, band, orchestra, technical staff, or worship team. In this community of people connected through ministry purpose, we do more than prepare songs and services—we engage hearts in message and theology. We pray, we sing, and we worship together.

I often tell choirs or teams I lead that God does a work *in* us before he does a work *through* us. If we are not a worshipping community, we will not lead our churches well in worship.

A third circle represents the *entire congregation of our church.* We engage them during the corporate times of worship—we sing, pray, give, testify, and respond, all to build up and encourage one another and to encounter our King and Lord, Jesus himself, to hear all he wants to say to us.

A fourth and largest circle is *outside the walls of our churches.* It represents the lost, the unreached people of the community and world. Worship ministries engage those people by inspiring and equipping a community of worshippers who love Jesus deeply and take the gospel that they sing to the world where they live. Our worship should always inspire us to tell the story of Jesus.

All four circles are essential to a vibrant worship ministry that makes disciples. A true disciple-making worship ministry focuses on all of them. An unhealthy imbalance results when a ministry stops short of all of them.

But just how does music help make disciples? Are we only talking about worship experiences?

No. And this is why it matters so much that we do these four circles well.

The correlation between how people think and what they sing is astounding to examine. In medical and scientific communities, much has been learned about the links between music, memory, attitude, and emotion. Unique in God's creation, people are wired to create melody and rhythm and link them to thought and reason. And when those come together, something amazing happens to the souls of mankind. We are moved to action and stirred to response.

Filmmakers know this. That's why they put music scores in movies. Even in the age of silent pictures, someone would play a piano in the theater. Educators know this. That's why we learned the alphabet by singing a song. Parents know this. That's why we use songs to teach simple skills to our young children.

And church leaders should know this too. The songs our people sing become the prayers our people will pray in their moments of deepest crisis. The expression of worship from the heart of God's people turns into songs of worship sung in the congregation, in the waiting room of a hospital, and yes, even at the bedside of a soldier going home to be with the Lord.

Many if not most people will forget the points of our sermons, but almost all will remember the songs we sing. It can be argued that much of what our people know and believe about God will come from what we sing in church. And notice I said *sing* and not *hear*. Only hearing these songs fails to produce the same effects as singing them. Because this is true, what we sing and how we sing in church matters a great deal to all of us.

God gave us the gift of music. And with it, we can inform and inspire. We can take truths about God that transform hearts and lock those truths into our souls by singing them back and forth over each other. Together, we can praise our God with songs of devotion and adoration from the deepest places of ourselves—heart, soul, mind. That's what worship is and what Jesus called for from all of us in Matthew 22:37.

Can worship be part of discipleship? The answer is a resounding yes! It is an essential part of the growth and development of healthy disciples.

Two Leaders, One Ministry

It was the great Christian apologist John Lennox who said, "Worship is a response to the revelation of God." We have often thought of Proverbs 29:18 as a verse about visionary leadership because it is often quoted this way: "Where there is no vision, the people perish" (KJV). The Christian Standard Bible gives us a wonderful rendering of this verse that brings more clarity to the meaning:

> Without revelation people run wild,
> but one who follows divine instruc-
> tion will be happy. (Prov. 29:18)

In other words, in places where the Word of God is absent, the people will live aimlessly. Our living is our everyday worship, so revelation—the proclamation of the Word of God—is an essential part of worship.

But so is our response. The Bible addresses singing more than one hundred times and praise many more times than that. Whenever God is revealed through his Word in the person of Jesus Christ, people who understand who he is will respond in worship.

That is what our gatherings should be all about—revelation and response.

The pastor and the singer are two leaders doing one thing—leading worship—and both are involved in revelation and response. Worship leadership is a shared ministry.

If this is true, the way these leaders engage with each other will affect their connection in leading worship. I want to suggest three ways these two leaders can share this ministry.

Shared ministry requires shared vision.

What should our worship services be like? How will we measure impact? What opportunities should we give our people for response? These are just a few of the questions these leaders can explore continually.

Shared ministry requires shared preparation.

Years ago I began to study what my pastor was studying. If he was preparing a series on Ephesians, I started doing my own study of the book. Then in our meetings I would ask him questions about his approach and what he planned to emphasize from the text. I wanted to read the books influencing him and discuss them together. I listened to the preachers I knew he loved to hear.

I also gave him recordings of songs I felt could be strategic for our ministry and asked him to share his thoughts. I wanted to be in his headspace, and I wanted him to be in mine. When we met, we had a shared preparation for our planning together.

Shared ministry requires shared execution.

Sure, these two leaders can theoretically execute their individual plans without the input of the other. But how much stronger can this shared ministry be if the two execute their vision together each week?

A review of previous worship services and planning for future ones with an emphasis on execution will benefit both leaders. There should be a rhythm of planning and evaluating all the time. Great trust can grow in these meetings.

I am confident of this—churches that are led by a pastor and music leader who share the worship ministry greatly benefit from the synergy their relationship brings. Many church members will not be able to articulate this, but they will know their worship leaders are on the same page leading a shared ministry.

Mission and Strategy

Churches have a mission. Healthy churches have a clear understanding of the mission and look at everything they do through the lens of whether or not it is mission critical. If a program accomplishes the mission, it is given priority.

Though you will see it stated many different ways in different contexts, the mission of a New Testament church is simple: make disciples. The worship ministry that only pursues musical or artistic objectives may hit them all, only to find in the end that there was no contribution to the mission.

A "worship war" is really just a symptom of the much deeper problem of putting the focus on strategy instead of mission. Whenever strategy becomes the focus of a ministry, the potential for disagreement and conflict grows exponentially.

The mission is to make disciples. The strategy can be the kind of music we choose, whether or not we use choirs or smaller vocal teams, and if we wear choir robes or not. The strategy will change year to year and over and over again. We should never marry our strategy.

But the mission doesn't change. It's been the same since Jesus called the first disciples with "Follow me" and commanded every believer since with "Go and make disciples." Leaders who can connect the dots of strategy with the larger mission of the church will enjoy deeper conversations with church leaders than "I don't like the drums."

I had one of those conversations with a man named Doug.

Doug was a senior adult in our church. He had been a faithful part of that congregation for forty years and was thought of as a supporter of all the church was doing. He was frequently involved in missions, going on short-term trips or sponsoring others to go when he couldn't go himself. No one thought of him as a troublemaker.

So imagine my surprise when he approached me after a morning service and said, "I don't like our music." Thankfully, the Lord gave me one of those moments of maturity that eluded me in my earlier churches. I replied, "Well, if you can't believe in what I'm doing, can you believe in what I'm trying to do? And, if you'll let me, I'd like to buy you a cup of coffee this week and explain what I think God is leading me to do in our church in worship."

The next morning, I was sitting in Doug's office with a cup of coffee from a local coffee shop. I spent the next hour explaining how the mission of making disciples was driving the strategy in the songs I was choosing, the role our choirs had in the equation, and how the flow of our worship gatherings were designed to engage people in the discipleship process.

He had good questions and helped me clarify the strategy as I heard him out. And his view of what I was doing started changing as he heard me out. When I left that morning, our church had two new people in it: a worship pastor with a better picture of how my choices were impacting a significant part of our congregation, and a senior adult leader who was now an advocate and voice of support for the strategies of our worship ministry. When I left that church a few years later, Doug was the last person in the line of people saying goodbye.

Part of a Team

The worship ministry can be made up of "those folks" who do the music thing that keep to themselves and are somewhat isolated from the rest of the church. The worship pastor can be the guy who argues over the budget, demands first consideration in every calendar meeting, and contends for the people resources with every other ministry of the church. In those settings, choirs become marginal, and pockets of resentment develop in a congregation that sits and stares at the musicians.

Or, this leader and ministry can be part of a team that has a single mission: making disciples. They naturally fit into a team of people with the same mission and learn the joy of serving others in pursuit of the goal.

Great worship ministry leaders understand the connection and find ways to articulate and model the mission no matter what changes in strategy come along.

CHAPTER SIX

ARTISTS AND SHEPHERDS

Understanding the ministry of worship leading has certainly been a process over the course of my life. I was thirteen years old when I first began to articulate a deep conviction that God had called me to serve him through music, and ever since that day, I have tried to understand what is involved in the role of leading worship.

First, a little history.

In 1980, I stepped into Calvary Baptist Church in Cleveland, Mississippi, to fill the part-time role of "minister of music and youth." I understood that it was my responsibility to select the hymns for worship, prepare the choirs and musicians to sing and play, organize activities for the children and youth of the church, and assist the pastor with various other duties, as he would assign them. It all seemed pretty simple to me.

This was back in an era when the church sang from a very selected, pre-approved set of hymns and songs found in the hymnal. Christian music as we know it today was something you would only hear in a concert or on the radio. The idea that the church would sing the same songs sung by Christian artists was foreign to our way of thinking then.

There were no lyrics of songs projected onto screens in the sanctuary and no "praise team" singing out in front of the choir. Occasionally, we would print the lyrics of a chorus in the bulletin, but by and large, the hymnal was the source of all of our congregational music. As a result, it was uncommon to sing very many new songs. We sang hymns that we had sung all of our lives—or at least since 1975, when those hymns were introduced in that edition of the Baptist hymnal. This same approach was true in many churches.

I was already playing the guitar, and occasionally I would lead worship accompanying the church myself. This gave me a freedom to throw in songs not found in the hymnal. Even then, the contrast between me, a "minister of music," and the "Christian artist" on the radio, was obvious. I was leading congregational worship and the artist was singing songs about Jesus for edification of the church. Both were important, but no one confused the two.

Then projectors and transparencies came into the sanctuary.

Companies like Maranatha and Integrity Hosanna began to write, record, and publish a different kind of song for Christians—songs that believers wanted to sing together in worship. The young people of the "Jesus Movement" in the late sixties and early seventies were now adults leading churches. The Christian folk song that defined that generation's spiritual development was making its way from the bonfires of youth retreats into the Sunday morning worship services of churches.

At the same time, the rise of the Christian Music Industry was taking hold. Virtually every iconic artist in the secular music scene had a counterpart in Christian music. From 1980–2000, bands were on tour, albums were flying off the shelves of stores, and the "Golden Age of Christian Music" was in full bloom. The Christian music segment became a market that secular companies invested in because of the enormous opportunity for sales.

In his book *We Will Stand*, author and music executive Stan Moser recalls the early days of Christian music and the iconic artists who inspired young people across the world to express their faith in a music style that sounded like their own generation. He writes, "Looking back on this era, it seems like God was moving so powerfully through Contemporary Christian Music that we just had to show up to succeed. In the sales department we adopted the motto, 'Stock 'em high and watch 'em buy!'"[13]

A young person who was passionate about music and was writing and singing songs of faith could easily imagine a career as a Christian artist. And there were many who did that very thing. Artists like DeGarmo and Key, David Meece, Steven Curtis Chapman, the Imperials, and many more burst on the scene in the late '70s and '80s. In the '90s, Christian music became such a big part of American culture that Christian artists like Michael W. Smith and Amy Grant crossed over into popular markets. They, along with Sandi Patti and others, made appearances on *The Tonight Show* and other popular entertainment programs. Their dreams were big and their opportunities were bigger.

Enter the iPod.

In 2001, Apple icon Steve Jobs walked out onto a stage and held up a device no one had ever seen before. On it, a person could store digital files of music to play, replay, organize, and much more. But where would these songs come from? They came from a source called iTunes. And how much would a song cost? Ninety-nine cents per song.

The music industry yawned at this development without realizing a nail had been driven in their business coffin. At the time this happened, a full artist CD would sell for $17.99 and include ten songs, or $1.80 per song. If a person wanted an album with a particular song, he or she had to buy the whole album to get it, meaning those songs were worth far more. Now with the arrival of the iPod, songs could be acquired one at a time and for half the price. The digital revolution had begun, and the music business would never be the same.

Christian artists could no longer support themselves with record sales, and all of this was happening at the same time contemporary songs were finding their way into our worship. So where did all the artists go?

They landed on the stages of our churches. Meanwhile, back at the choir room . . .

Churches began to celebrate the new music coming from the worship generation by writing new songs, developing a band and worship team approach to congregational singing, and filling choir lofts with drum sets, green plants, and décor instead of choirs.

The hymnals became doorstops, guitars replaced organs, and new songs replaced the ones previous generations had sung for decades.

This Is a Good Thing—or Is It?

Many great things happened along the way. Artists brought their artistry to the church, and the church benefited from it. Churches began to invest in better technology and more capable technical support of worship services. The sounds began to appeal to a wider age group of people. Churches wanted to produce a higher quality music experience.

A new kind of song started to emerge—one that expressed more emotion and more personal kinds of response. The songs were simpler, more repetitive, and easier to learn. Every Sunday could have that "youth camp" kind of atmosphere.

But over time, it began to take a different shape. The songs started sounding the same.

The group of people leading became smaller and smaller in number and the gap between what we used to do and what we are doing now got wider and wider. Technologies started coming into the worship visually, and lighting became a worship component.

Our sound systems got better. And slowly— even unintentionally—the focus of our singing shifted from the pew to the stage. The disposition of the person in the congregation went from "I'm here to sing" to "I'm here to listen."

This is a good thing, right? Artists want people to listen and people want to listen, so what is wrong with that?

Filling Stations and Altars

Passive congregations indicate a problem with our mind-set about worship.

Ever heard someone say something like this to the pastor? "You've got to feed me today, Pastor. I had a really hard week and feel pretty empty this morning. I'll need a great service to get me ready for next week." Or, someone else might say, "I like listening to the music on Sunday. It really feeds my soul."

It's a mind-set you'll hear expressed often at church in one form or another. And if you think about it, this mind-set suggests that Christians should come to church to *get something*. They bring a set of expectations and, if those aren't met, leave disappointed and even critical. Church for them is a *filling station* only there to fill their empty tanks for the next week.

That's not how the Bible characterizes church.

The spiritual discipline of corporate worship is characterized in the Bible with words like *sacrifice* and *submission*. It takes the posture of *humility* and *surrender* with hands that are raised up—not out. When we think like this, worship becomes a place we go to *give something*.

It started in Genesis with Abel and Abraham, goes to Moses and through David, and culminates all the way to a hill outside Jerusalem where the ultimate act of worship was modeled on a cross. Jesus' call to the disciples is not, "Come follow me and you'll get everything you need." It is "Take up your cross, die to yourself, and follow me."

It's about dying—to one's ambition and pride and self-righteousness. It's about laying down your preferences and sacrificing your interests. It requires giving away your rights and privileges and submitting yourself to the authority of God's

Word and expressing submission in self-abandonment. And, yes, one of those ways of expression commanded in Scripture is "singing."

A *Filling Station* worship experience is one where you go to *get* something—it's about you.

An *Altar* worship experience is one where you go to *give* yourself for something—it's about the glory of God.

Many believers have it backwards. Worship shouldn't be measured by how much we receive. Believers shouldn't come to church empty to be filled up for the next week. We come full, because of our daily walk with Jesus and his work in our lives through the week. By the time Sunday comes, we are so full of gratitude for his faithfulness and goodness that we can't wait to join the rest of the body of Christ and empty out our praise on Jesus. Then we leave empty to be filled again as we walk in unity with Christ through the week.

Filling station worship focuses on my needs being met. *Altar* worship focuses on my sacrifice being given.

Do We Need Artists or Shepherds?

Yes.

Leadership in the church has many facets, and the Bible has much to say about it. From the description of elders in 1 Timothy 3 and Titus 1 to the instructions to pastors in Ephesians 4 and 1 Peter, we see a clear picture of what ministry leadership looks like.

The Greek verb *poimaino* ("to shepherd") is the basis for most of these texts. Paul and Peter use it extensively in their descriptions of leading God's people. The image applies to worship ministry as well.

Artists sing *for* the sheep; shepherds *teach* the sheep to sing.

Artists lead the sheep *with* something; shepherds lead the sheep *to* something.

Artists *express* their artistry (which can be worshipful); shepherds *lead* the sheep to express their worship.

You get the idea.

The truth of the matter is, we need both artists and shepherds in our communities of believers. We need artists who are creating and expressing our wonder, our worship of our God. We need artists who inspire the beautiful and aesthetic expressions that declare the beauty and awesome nature of our God.

Healthy worship ministries understand that our music should be excellent. The existence of art itself reflects the majesty of the God we serve. The church needs artists who pursue excellence in that expression and inspire the rest of us to pursue it as well. The song God hears is one song from all of us. The artists among us enhance our praise with their artistry.

By myself, I'm an okay singer. But put me next to Charles Billingsley and we're pretty special together. Artists bring joy to all of us as they contribute their abilities to inspire the worship of God's people.

But we must have shepherds. These are the leaders who understand that our music is more than art to be expressed—it is a tool to be used for the benefit of the sheep.

What's the Difference?

When artists lead our worship, we can unintentionally foster a *Filling Station* worship culture. Over the last two decades, ministers of music started "aging out" and Christian artists were taking their places. Pastors started looking for someone just to "do the music." The expectations of the worship leader became more narrow and centered on performance. Ministries that required administration—choirs, children's music, student choirs—all began to disappear, mostly because the artists were not equipped to lead them.

Church leaders began to associate church growth with a contemporary music style and did everything they could to move to that approach as quickly as possible. But musical changes without the spiritual shepherding of a pastor only led to division and confusion.

And sadly, in many settings, the "Worship Wars" had begun.

We need a new kind of leader—one who has learned the language of music well, but also clearly understands the calling of disciple-making that rests on the church. These are individuals who excel in their craft, but understand their role of worship-leading to be spiritual in nature.

More than talent, they have a calling.

More than skills, they have servant hearts.

They love music, but they love people more.

They are disciples who make disciples.

We need artistic shepherds.

VALUE THREE

ENGAGE THE BODY

CHAPTER SEVEN

ENGAGING THE BODY OF CHRIST

Worship is hard to measure on Sundays. It may be even impossible. We look around the gathering of people and try to determine whether or not the people are actually worshipping God, and we have no idea if what we think is happening is really happening.

I realized years ago that real worship, the kind that Paul talks about in Romans 12:1, is best measured on all the days of the week, not just on Sundays. Why? Listen to his definition of worship: "Present your bodies as a living sacrifice, holy and pleasing to God; this is your true worship." Notice, there's nothing specifically about singing there, nor is there anything specific about Sundays. There is certainly something special about corporate worship, but overall, worship is defined as sacrificing ourselves for God and his purposes all the time.

Therefore, worship is best measured by the ways we do our work, lead our families, and serve our neighbors. It's about our love for God, our love for his people, and our love for the lost. It really doesn't have much to do with how well the worship set went last Sunday.

And yet, the Bible clearly teaches us to sing. Churches with healthy worship cultures don't settle for anything less.

In his book *True Worshipers*, Bob Kauflin writes, "No one is excused. Not even those with zero musical ability. The critical question is not, 'Do I have a voice?' But rather, 'Do I have a song?'"[14] Many years ago, Buddy Earwood, my minister of music growing up and my mentor in ministry, would often ask the same questions. "Are you a Christian? Then sing the song you have been given to sing!"

In Scripture, singing was assigned and carried out. The psalmist testifies, "He put a new song in my mouth, a hymn of praise to our God" (Ps. 40:3). Psalm 107 describes this process in detail: "Let the redeemed of the LORD proclaim that he has redeemed them" (v. 2). The psalm goes on to identify four groups of people who called out to God in their distress—he hears them and delivers them, and then they join the song of the redeemed.

Consider the lyric to the great hymn by Fanny Crosby, "Blessed Assurance":

> *This is my story, this is my song, praising my Savior all the day long.*

Singing Runs in the Family of Faith

Worship is an inward disposition with outward expressions, and there is no single outward expression that proves the heart is worshipping. The person singing every song with hands in the air may not be worshipping. The one that never opens his mouth or moves in any way externally may be the one standing in God's throne room. We just can't tell.

And yet, we are commanded to sing in the assembly of the redeemed. Healthy worship cultures set the value of congregational engagement far above any artistic quality or accomplishment.

Hebrews 13:15 says, "Therefore, through him let us continually offer up to God a sacrifice of praise, that is, the fruit of our lips that confess his name."

What Happened?

If God puts the song of praise into the mouths of the redeemed and if he directs and instructs us to sing and give him praise, why does congregational singing seem to be a diminishing characteristic of many of our churches? What happened?

My role at LifeWay Worship gives me the unique opportunity to see and hear about what many different churches are doing in their worship and music ministries. To be sure, there are many churches filled with enthusiastic singers, but generally speaking, our people do not sing like our parents and grandparents did. And even worse, the leaders of those churches don't seem to know it.

In many of our churches today, our music has become very produced with visual enhancements and top sound reinforcement. That's not a bad thing—in fact, it can be a great thing! But when the stage lighting effects dominate the experience, the leaders on stage cannot even see the faces of their congregation. It amuses me when a leader has to put his hand over his eyes to try and see his people. That indicates a major issue to me; if we gather corporately to be inspired as individuals by the singing of all, it is problematic that the leader can't even hear what the room is singing! Add to that a highly produced sound mix with in-ear monitors and a full stage mix in the floor monitors, and, well, they can't hear them either.

So, if we cannot see or hear the congregation, how would we know that the people have stopped singing? It would do any pastor or worship leader a world of good to spend a service just watching the people. They might be surprised—and disappointed.

Here are several reasons why many worshippers have stopped singing:

They don't know the song.

As we grow in our faith and mature in our worship expressions, new songs find their way into our worship and bring new clarity to our faith. But, in many churches, there is such a focus on the latest new song that the familiar is overlooked. People like to sing songs they know and songs that resonate with them.

They can't sing the song.

A common concern voiced these days is that songs are too high for the average churchgoer to sing well. Do people sing lower than they used to? I suspect not. I think the problem rests in the way a song gets to the church these days. Many songs go straight from the Christian artist's recording to the worship service. Often the key sung by the artist translates right into the arrangement sung by the church, and very often, it just doesn't work.

There are practical and musical reasons why this is true: the melody is often in the upper register of the tenor voice, making it too low for sopranos. Consequently, sopranos are forced to sing alto (something they don't like to do), or sing in their upper register (watch out if you're sitting in front of them!) or, sadly, drop out. Bass lines are often left out of new songs, eliminating many of the men in the worship service. In a generation when engaging men in the life of the church is already difficult, we should not make it more challenging by singing songs most of them can't sing.

But it goes deeper than key. Often newer songs have rhythms that don't lend themselves to congregational singing and, rather than struggle, the worshipper will just quit. They may love the song; they just can't sing it, especially if they barely know it. As they become more and more familiar with a song, they can handle harder rhythms.

Another reason they can't sing the song is one of the few downsides of projecting lyrics to songs. The congregation may never see the notes to a song and be forced to pick it up over time by rote. Often, by the time they catch on to it, the worship leader has moved on to new songs and no longer sings the one they struggled to learn.

They can't hear the room singing.

The typical person in the pew is not in love with their own voice. But if they can be part of something larger, where their individual voice is not distinguishable, they will sing with enthusiasm. In today's rhythm-driven worship, so dependent on sound reinforcement, the decibel level often gets higher and higher. When this happens, the individual worshipper can hear only two things: the sound coming through the system and their own voice. They cannot hear the sound of the congregation singing—the part they can "hide" their voice inside. In other words, a person with very little singing confidence will still sing with gusto if they can hear the rest of the room singing as they sing, and their voice doesn't stand out to them. Without the confidence that comes when the whole room can be heard, many of our people will just stop singing.

There certainly are times when the volume in an exciting, energetic service should be on the loud side. The problem comes when it is constantly at that level. If the individual cannot hear the whole room singing, they will feel like they stick out—in fact, they do stick out to themselves. And that is the average worshipper's worst nightmare. This happens when the sound is too loud, especially if the band, choir, and vocal team are at full strength.

A very easy way to improve this dynamic is to turn the sound down and sing with a variety of accompaniments (including a cappella). Let the congregation "win" when they sing and watch their confidence (and their singing) get better and better.

They think they are not expected to sing or needed in the worship.

You've probably seen churches where everything about their worship space—lighting, sound, and stage—screams, "We don't expect you to participate—sit back, relax, and enjoy your worship ride."

How does that happen? When the congregation is sitting in the dark, and the performers on stage are presented in theatrical lighting effects, the church may actually be saying to the congregation they have come to watch something. And, if that is what it seems to say, that's what they will do.

Lighting can contribute to a great worship atmosphere, but it can also be a hindrance to participation if not carefully planned.

A vibrant worship ministry considers every variable. They ask questions like, "What does our stage arrangement and lighting say about what we expect our congregation to do?" and "How does the way we use technology enhance or hinder congregational engagement?"

If they are sitting in the dark with a blacked-out ceiling and tour-like stage lighting effects, singing songs they don't know, accompanied by a loud, artistically styled mix of sound, and a feature "artist" throwing in every vocal lick under the sun, well . . . you get the point. They are not going to sing, because in their hearts they know you don't really want them to.

They don't trust their leadership.

In one season of leading worship ministry, I was guilty of an attitude that negatively affected the way the congregation engaged in worship. It took months of frustration and soul-searching to realize that my attitude was creating a barrier for the congregation.

During this experience I learned that I couldn't plan and lead worship with an agenda.

The attitude—though I didn't really realize it at the time—was that I was there to use my skill to rescue the church from their traditional worship. I was "transitioning" them to more current styles of music and more contemporary responses of worship. Every Sunday, every song, I was training them to worship the way I thought they were supposed to worship—with the music I liked and the energy that matched my personality. I selected songs that displayed my strengths and abilities. Secretly, I often thought the church was really fortunate to have me as their leader.

When people didn't like something, I wrote it off as their problem and assumed they just didn't "get it." I justified that attitude by explaining I couldn't be bothered with the "naysayers." I was focused on the mission of "fixing the worship," so I continued changing the music style of the church to fit my agenda. I was in a battle, and I was going to win!

Two years later, I had learned the hard way that people will not follow a leader with an agenda like that one.

Going through this experience helped me realize I couldn't develop a healthy worship culture through a musical change. It required becoming a spiritual leader, one who had spiritual credibility, and not just performing as an artist who would dismiss any person who didn't get the groove. It required serving people and taking extra care with those who were struggling with new songs and new worship experiences. I had to die to my "bag of tricks" and start praying and leading with a spiritual focus. I had to start building bridges and climbing walls—I even had to blow up a few walls that I'd built myself.

They will never say it this way, but people in a church can tell when their leaders are taking them somewhere they are not sure they want to go. And if you have that agenda, no matter how noble what you are doing may seem, you will not be leading God's people. You'll only be leading a cause for yourself.

The Cost of an Unengaged Congregation

I heard someone say recently, "What difference does it make? Do people really have to sing in order to worship? Why can't the singers sing, and everyone else just listen and worship?" Years ago, I might have said the same thing.

But now I believe losing this time-honored part of church practice has cost us far more than we realize.

The Bible clearly describes two types of worship experiences for the believer: private and corporate. No matter what is happening on the stage, the individual can worship in a corporate setting even if the body as a whole is not participating, that's for sure. But I fear when we create a passive environment in corporate worship where the only expected response from the whole is to listen, we lull our people into being passive about all the aspects of the corporate experience—in how they listen, and sadly, how they respond to the call of God on their lives. And passive worshippers, I'm afraid, leave our buildings Sunday after Sunday to live as passive Christians in a world that desperately needs them to be anything but passive.

But in those places where the entire congregation is actively involved in the corporate experience, they hear more, express more, and understand more about what God is saying and expecting in response. They respond more to him and his call on their lives. The worship experiences of their church encourage engagement in a world that desperately needs to know the unique nature of our Lord, the one we worship, Jesus Christ.

Isn't that the goal of the corporate worship event?

Beyond that, if worship leaders make participation difficult for the congregation, we are actually hindering the spiritual growth of the people we serve. As believers, they are commanded to sing—why would we make that harder than it has to be? Why not make every effort and concession to ensure the most people can follow through in obedience to the biblical command to sing?

It Really Is This Simple

Healthy congregational worship ministries place a high value on congregational engagement. When they evaluate the impact of this work, they consider the active involvement of the people in the worship gathering to be one of the key metrics to consider.

Do they pursue excellence in music performance? Yes. But that alone is never enough for these ministries. If their music is great but their congregation is not involved, they don't consider it a win.

The easiest way to address this immediately would be these simple adjustments: turn the lights up and the volume down, and pick songs and hymns that are familiar to the church. Use new songs with intentionality. Make every choice about engagement—the key, the style, and the type of accompaniment.

When planning music for the congregation, put them first—not your own interests, but theirs.

When the church starts singing again, you will find smaller issues will start to fade. You will gain more trust from the congregation and feel more freedom to lead them as you grow together in worship.

It was Harold Best who said, "The human voice, given over to Jesus, and found in community with other voices given over similarly, produces a dignified and worthy song from storefront church to cathedral."[15] He goes on to say, "We do not go to church to worship. But as continuing worshipers, we gather ourselves together to continue to worship, but now in the company of brothers and sisters."[16]

The Bible has much to say about corporate worship. Here are just a few of the references instructing us about corporate worship:

Come, let us worship and bow down.
(Ps. 95:6a)

Let the word of Christ dwell richly
among you, teaching and admonishing
one another through psalms, hymns,
and spiritual songs . . . (Col. 3:16a)

I will praise you, LORD, among the
peoples. (Ps. 108:3a)

The references to the corporate nature of worship permeate the Scriptures in both the Old and
New Testaments, culminating in Revelation with
the description of the eternal scene of the bride
of Christ singing the new song of worship at the
marriage feast of the Lamb (Rev. 5). No one will
be sitting there with their mouths closed and their
arms folded.

The teaching is clear. There is no substitute
for the collective song of worship from the body of
Christ. Worship leaders have the great privilege
of leading the song of faith in the assembly of the
saints. That we all join in singing it should be an
identifying mark of the worship we lead.

CHAPTER EIGHT

WORSHIP DESEGREGATION

It's a beautiful day to sit outside and work on a book—so that's exactly what I decided to do. As I write this, two fathers, each with their own four-year-old son, are enjoying our neighborhood pool just fifty feet away from me. The whole scene floods my mind with great memories of that season of my life.

One father picks up his son and throws him in the air, then carefully guiding him down until a huge splash welcomes him back to the water. Now the other boy says, "Me too!" and his father does the same thing. The best part of all is when the boys "surprise" their dads with a splash of water—then the dads retaliate with another round of throwing the boys into the pool.

Conspicuously, both dads are standing at the very place in the pool where the water gets deeper, and the danger to the young swimmers becomes real. Every "son-throw" goes toward the shallow end.

There's something really right about the whole scene.

Know Where the Danger Lies

Besides having a whole lot of fun, these boys very much need to learn how to take care of themselves in the water. Between moments of play, the dads are giving small instructions, and slowly, the young boys are becoming more and more comfortable in the pool. Before long, these guys will be swimming like fish.

How does this happen? It starts with dads making an important decision. Instead of spending the afternoon playing golf or skiing on the lake with their buddies, these fathers decided to take their sons to the pool.

It seems to be a pretty obvious analogy—for the dads to teach their sons how to swim, they have to be in the pool together. Fast-forward twenty-five years from now and it's likely this scene will be repeated, as the sons of today become the fathers of tomorrow.

Watching these fathers prompts this question in my heart, *Where and from whom will our children learn how to worship God?*

Parents are eager for their children to learn many things: how to swim, how to ride a bike, and how to read. Do the parents in our churches understand their critical role in teaching their children how to worship?

And pondering all that leads me to this question, *Why in the world would we segregate generations in worship?*

How Did We Get Here?

I'm convinced we didn't intend for this to happen.

When we began to get outside the hymnal and introduce new songs in worship, a stirring happened in the church. For the first time, there were songs finding their way into the worship that many worshippers didn't know, with instruments we weren't used to in church. It was exciting to bring new songs into the worship services of our churches! But, very soon, a divide began to surface.

In many churches, we decided to start a new service, not just for space reasons, but so we could plan different types of music in each service, (hopefully) believing that using different music styles in different services would settle down the conflict caused by the introduction of contemporary songs in worship.

And, for a long time, it seemed to be working.

But over time something else began to happen. People began to migrate to the worship service that best fit their generation. The discipleship ministry of the church began to follow suit by organizing the Bible study hour around the generational divide. In some of our churches, we took this model even further by starting a Kid's Worship experience that moved our children into a different service. Student and College ministries did the same thing in some of these churches.

Without meaning to, we isolated the generations of our churches from each other, robbing parts of the body from the other parts that the Bible says they desperately need, and we did it all in the name of protecting our "unity" from the rise of musical preferences. In the name of unity, we fractured our churches.

Blended Is the Answer, Right?

One of my favorite Twitter accounts to follow is The Church Curmudgeon. A few years ago, I had the privilege to meet the humorous guy behind the account and we have since become friends. It turns out he's a minister of music in a church, which helped me understand quickly why he was so clever in his "curmudgeon-isms." Why wouldn't someone who walks through this valley of balancing the music of a diverse congregation be equipped to recount the real and imagined humorous quips of his flock.

Here are a few of my favorites about worship from his book *Then Tweets My Soul*:

- Worship team practice is cancelled. Use the four chords from last week.
- I may not agree with your choice of worship music, but I'll defend to the death your right to stop playing it.
- Worship leader is going to explain to the seniors why he doesn't do hymns. Or, "Singer in the Hands of an Angry Mob."

- There is no "I" in team. Unless it's the worship team then it's every other word.

And, my personal favorite . . .

- Worship team practice tonight. They'll be working on new arrangements of old hymns so the seniors can hate them too.[17]

Even through humor, the point is well made. Music—by itself—can wreak havoc in an otherwise healthy fellowship of Christians.

Divided generations is not the only problem we created while trying to unify the church through music. In places where starting a new service wasn't the best option, we started trying to "blend" our worship, to take the "we will have something for everyone" approach to worship planning.

In this model, we plan worship with a template—one that is viewable and sharable and known by all. It goes something like this:

> We always have at least one hymn accompanied by organ and piano, one worship song with band, one choir selection (without vocal team),

and a welcome song that can be a praise chorus. And we have the bulletins in the archives to prove it.

Man, that sounds exciting.

Now, there's nothing wrong with variety in worship. As a matter of fact, the Bible clearly demonstrates variety in music and goes nowhere near instituting a template for instrumentation or song style—quite the opposite.

There Has to Be a Better Way

There is.

Creating a healthy worship culture means setting the value of worship as a spiritual discipline above any and all music preferences. It means shepherding a group of people in such a way that they genuinely care about each other. It means developing the spiritual maturity of the congregation so that they think beyond templates and music styles.

It takes all generations to foster a healthy, disciple-making, legacy-building community of faith. Music becomes a tool that facilitates this process, but it is not, nor could it ever be, the key to holding a community of believers together.

Churches that create a generationally segregated congregation through music preferences are only delaying inevitable disruption in the body's future, and they are doing so in the name of eliminating disruption in the present. Over time, the church grows further and further apart and consequently becomes an easy target for conflict over even the smallest of issues.

Fathers and Sons, Mothers and Daughters

Generational segregation in worship does more than create problems for churches. When we segregate age groups in worship, we are also disrupting the families in our churches. There are God-given responsibilities to parents for the development of their children that we undermine when we remove them from worship.

I love the worship at the church my family attends. We do a wide range of music with a variety of accompaniments that range from rhythm-driven modern songs to orchestra and choir-led anthems—and just about everything in between.

But one of the most meaningful parts of our morning worship doesn't involve music at all. It's a special time we call the "Prayer and Altar Time." During these moments, the congregation is invited to be still and reflective in a posture of prayer—no singing, usually with a piano playing very reflectively—and for those moments, it is quiet. We also invite anyone who would like to join the pastor at the altar to slip out of the pew and find a place on the steps. It is an important part of our worship services every week.

Recently, during one of these times in our church, I saw something that reinforced for me something I already knew to be true—fathers and mothers have a profound influence over their families. And much, if not most, of that influence has a great deal more to do with what we do than what we say, or thankfully, how we sound when we sing.

What did I see?

I saw a father slip out of the pew and come to the altar, and then his two sons follow right behind him. I would submit to anyone, no other human being on the planet can influence those two boys like that one dad can.

I have come to believe that, rather than merely articulating a godly vision to my children of the kind of people I would hope they will become, I ought to focus on being an example for them with the kind of person I am becoming myself. I ought to do in front of them the things I aspire for them to do.

I challenge you to watch any family at church. If the father sings, they all will sing. If Mom participates, the daughter will as well. If he or she prays, they all will pray. If they give, the children will give too.

But if Dad has his arms folded and remains passive, the whole family will likely yawn all the way through the service. Sadly, if the kids never worship with their families, all of this potential impact is lost. And no ministry can replace the impact the leaders of a family can have on their own children in worship.

It really is this simple—children follow their parents to the altar.

The Church at Station Hill

I am a part of Brentwood Baptist Church in Brentwood, Tennessee. Over the last few years, our church has strategically started and revitalized churches in key areas of population growth in middle Tennessee. One of those churches is The Church at Station Hill, located in Spring Hill. The pastor is Jay Strother.

This church, from its outset, decided that intergenerational discipleship would be in their DNA. The music and worship, led by Cliff Duren, reflects this strategy. Everywhere you look as this church worships you see families. Even in the choir loft or praise team, band, and technical staff, you see mothers and daughters, fathers and sons.

I asked Jay to outline for me why this strategy, particularly as to how it related to their worship ministry, was such a key part of what they do. This is what he said:

> The identity of a church is found in its worship gathering. We are all in agreement about the focus of our worship, that our worship should unite us around King Jesus. But I also believe that the way we worship matters. Worship is one of the most important ways the church is unified, and we should see our worship gatherings as an opportunity to further strengthen all generations rather than divide them. Ephesians 4:3 instructs us that the Spirit creates unity, but that we have to "contend" or "make every effort to keep" unity in our churches, and that call extends to the unity of all generations declaring together the

greatness of our God. Our identity as a people is that we are all one in Christ—regardless of age, standing in society, or ethnicity. Our worship gatherings should reflect this reality.

The best way to equip a generation to worship is to include them as full participants in the worshipping community. We bemoan the struggle for kids who are raised in the church leaving the church as they emerge into adulthood. Is it any wonder they have difficulty transitioning if they've always been in age-segregated gatherings with songs, stories, and videos cultivated for their unique preferences? When we only have age-segregated gatherings, are we pandering to preferences to drive our numbers in the present, or are we thinking long-term about how we make lifelong disciples of Jesus? We have to be careful to create authentic worshippers and not merely consumers of religious programming.

One of the most effective ways to equip a generation is to include

them in the full worship gathering—
yes, as participants with their moms
and dads, grandmas and grandpas,
neighbors and friends—but also as
servants, using their time, talent,
and testimonies from the platform as
well. By doing so, we teach them that
what we do as the church "gathered"
(Heb. 10:24–25) matters, and that we
value them enough that we want
them to be an important part of that
moment each week in the life of our
church.

Intergenerational worship is obe-
dient to the Scripture that instructs
us to pass on our rich faith. There
are numerous passages in Scripture
that instruct us to "tell a future generation the praiseworthy acts of the
LORD" (Ps. 78:4). Intergenerational
worship enables the entire worshipping community to remember
and retell both God's mighty acts
in redemptive history and also the
rich stories of grace that are an
important part of every church's own
story and mission. The children and

grandchildren in our churches need to hear the testimonies of how God has moved. The songs we choose to sing now are those they will remember long after our voices are silenced.

I think Jay may be on to something.

Another important voice speaking to the strengths of a multigenerational approach to worship ministry is Ray Jones. For years as he served as worship pastor of the Community Bible Church in San Antonio, Ray modeled how the generations could serve each other in worship. I asked him to share a few thoughts on the subject. Here is what he said:

> Multigenerational or intergenerational worship has a new name. It is now called discipleship. The Scripture is very direct about this concept and even tells us that the older should train up the younger. Multigenerational worship paints an accurate picture of all generations gathering under the banner of worship in unified purpose. Targeting a specific look and feel in worship (no matter if it is modern or traditional)

sends a message to the entire church that worship is not an inclusive ministry. If our demographic of eighteen to thirty-five are the only people allowed to lead, then a great question will need to be addressed. "Who is training the next generation of worshippers and worship leaders?"

The worship in our churches has been segregated long enough. Healthy worship ministries understand the power of a unified and spirited corporate gathering that transcends style and preferences for the greater good of families and ministries.

Paul told the church in multiple places to find agreement for the sake of unity in the body. It's time for the generations to prefer each other in worship to any style of music.

Now, back to watching those two boys learn how to swim. Way to go, dads.

VALUE FOUR

ASPIRE WITH PURPOSE

CHAPTER NINE

THE ENEMIES OF DISTRACTION

You can call church music leaders worship pastors. Or ministers of music. Or maybe, worship leader or music guy or gal.

But here's a title that really fits—The Enemies of Distractions.

Wait a Minute!

In a previous chapter, we espoused the virtues of the shepherd role in ministry and questioned how artists fit into our disciple-making mission. You could assume from that discussion that how we do our music doesn't matter in a spiritually charged worship ministry. You would be wrong if you did.

We know the power of music to influence people. We've seen how critical it is that what we say in song be biblically accurate and Spirit-led. We understand that music is a language to carry the message of the gospel to the souls of humanity.

But have you realized how much of a distraction it can be?

The worship ministry has many ways to distract from the mission of the church:

- The drums are too loud.
- The vocal team doesn't dress appropriately.
- No one knows the song, including the choir.
- The lyric slides are out of order.
- There is a misspelled word.
- An instrument is out of tune.
- Poor operation of technical equipment.

These are the obvious ones that just about anyone can spot. But what about issues like these?

- An individual on the leadership team is living an ungodly lifestyle.
- A performance is over-the-top and doesn't fit into the presentation.

- An individual enjoys the spotlight but doesn't participate in the overall life of the church.
- A bad attitude from someone who feels under-utilized.
- Strong disagreements about song choices.

I've received more than a few emails from pastors asking what to do with the following type of situations:

- Inappropriate social media posts or pictures by leaders
- Questionable types of clothing worn by musicians
- Key influencers on the worship team inviting others over to watch questionable movies or television shows
- Division in the church over the content/style of the music

And there is one layer further that is even harder to navigate:

- A lyric of a song cannot be easily defended from Scripture.

- A program or presentation diminishes resources without contributing spiritually.
- Leaders with musical abilities lack spiritual disciplines.
- Worship leaders are otherwise isolated from the church.
- Conflicts with other ministries over calendar, budgets, and people resources.

There are many more of these potential distractions in worship ministry. Some worship leaders might say, "That's not my job. I can't police the behavior of adults in the ministry I lead." Or how about, "It's a shame those people feel that way. I can't be concerned with the detractors."

I disagree. Not only can we—we must.

The gospel is why we sing, *period*. Possessing and presenting the clear and powerful truth of God's Word through Jesus Christ is the only reason we exist. If something hampers or distracts from that gospel, we had better eradicate it, and fast. We know that God's Word has the power to change the lives of the people we lead. How can we live with anything that would distract from it?

This Is a Really Big Deal!

Have you ever seen a church embroiled in these kinds of issues with their Worship Ministry? It can be a nightmare. Instead of a beautiful and loving gathering of believers finding great joy in the corporate expression of worship week after week, it becomes a community of people who cringe at every introduction of the songs. The frustration is palpable, though it may be unexpressed or even inconspicuous.

Every aspect of the gathering is affected. The people attend with dread as the pastor tries to ignore the issues long enough to focus on his text for the morning. The Bible study classes start with ten minutes of what everyone hated about the worship that day.

There might as well be a pre-service announcement informing the guests that people are dissatisfied with the music so the guests will know why it feels so odd during the worship time.

There is no joy.

There is no unity.

There is no power.

There is no worship.

And no one can focus on the gospel.

Distractions that erupt in the Worship Ministry hurt a church much more than most probably realize. Some might say, "Well, that's just a small problem for a few people." But these types of distractions have cascading ramifications that touch every part of a church's ministry.

Aspiring with Purpose

Consider this attribute of healthy worship ministries—they fight against unnecessary distractions. They aspire for excellence in everything, not for the sake of artistic achievement, but for the purpose of the gospel going forth unhindered. These ministries invest . . .

- In the spiritual and musical development of their worship leaders and volunteers
- In the technologies they utilize
- In the planning and execution of the details in the worship service
- In the planning of the rehearsal and cadence of preparation

They evaluate . . .

- The godliness of their leaders

- The preparation of their volunteers
- The performance value of their choirs, instrumentalists, technical operators, soloists, vocal team
- The content of their songs

They do not . . .

- Allow an individual to unnecessarily impact the ministry by attitudes or behaviors that go unchecked
- Ignore issues that create dissention
- Prefer songs over people
- Isolate themselves from other ministries or demand to be served by the rest of the church

These leaders understand that distractions like these compromise the "mission ready" posture of the church. Far more than just a fractured worship gathering, these issues create a fractured congregation and compromise the effectiveness of the church's mission.

Most of All, This

Mission grows out of worship. That's not my opinion; it's the model put forth in Scripture over and over again.

Isaiah sees Jesus, confesses his sin, and then says "Here am I, send me" (Isa. 6).

The woman at the well sees Jesus, he reveals to her that he is the Messiah, and then she runs into the village to bring everyone back to meet the man who knew her better than anyone (John 4).

After Peter and John saw Jesus, then they preached the gospel with power and healed a crippled man. When confronted by the religious leaders, they said, "We cannot help speaking about what we have seen and heard" (Acts 4 NIV).

Saul sees Jesus on the Damascus road, falls in blindness and rises in obedience, then becomes the apostle to the Gentiles, planting churches and writing the letters that became most of the New Testament (Acts 9–28).

Even in Matthew 28, the Great Commission is given in the context of what they were doing in verse 17. It reads, "When they saw him, they worshipped . . ."

Mission grows out of worship.

We can create programs and try to convince people to live for Christ and to be his ambassadors. We can preach, cajole, manipulate, and guilt people into service all we want. The results will be short-lived. But when our people worship—when they encounter Jesus and his Word, when they engage in pouring their praise out on him and responding to the Holy Spirit at work in their lives—they will join the mission. It is the natural response of the worshipper.

Hebrews 11:6 says, "Now without faith it is impossible to please God, since the one who draws near to him must first believe that he exists and that he rewards those who seek him." What does God want from us? The verse tells us: he wants us to draw near, to worship. When we draw near, all other disciplines of the disciple fall in line in response.

Anything that distracts from worship disrupts the mission of the church.

A Psalm That Says It All

Psalm 126 captures the connection between worship and mission beautifully. A Psalm of Ascent, this psalm had a special place in the heart of the families traveling to Jerusalem for the feasts as they would sing it and say it along the way to God's place of worship. The origin of the psalm dates back to Ezra's day and possibly was written by Ezra. It tells the story of the second wave of exiles returning to Jerusalem from the Babylonian captivity.

> When the LORD restored the fortunes of Zion, we were like those who dream. (v. 1)

The Lord was "restoring the fortunes" of Zion with the return of the exiles. The "fortunes" in the psalm are the people that have been set free. God restored them when he delivered them from their captors.

> Our mouths were filled with laughter then, and our tongues with shouts of joy. Then they said among the nations, "The LORD has done great things for them." The LORD had done great things; we were joyful. (vv. 2–3)

Their deliverance brought joy and shouts of praise that when observed by others caused the nations to declare, "The LORD has done great things for them." It is an example of how our joyful worship, offered in response to God's deliverance in our lives, causes others to take notice.

> Restore our fortunes, LORD, like watercourses in the Negev. Those who sow in tears will reap with shouts of joy. (vv. 4–5)

This phrase seems out of place in the psalm. How could tears invade the song of joy? They do, because this is a prayer, coming from the heart of the delivered, for the "fortunes" yet to be restored. Worship produces this response in the worshipper. The expression, "I've been delivered! Praise the Lord!" in worship leads to a conviction in the heart of the worshipper: "There are still those who have not been delivered." The tears follow and the burden for the lost is unleashed on a heart full of God.

We see that this prayer in Psalm 126 is an echo of the one in Nehemiah 1. There, Nehemiah hears news from home, goes immediately into prayer and worship with God, and responds with a willingness to lead the rest of the exiles home to repair the walls.

> Though one goes along weeping, carrying the bag of seed, he will surely come back with shouts of joy, carrying his sheaves. (v. 6)

The cycle concludes with a new harvest of the delivered now adding to the shouts of joy. In the heart of a healthy church, it happens over and over again.

Worship produces mission that produces worship that produces mission—on and on and on it goes.

A church that does not have a rhythm of worship and mission may do many great things in its ministries, but, they will never be the church God wants them to be until this rhythm is established.

There is much at stake in our worship. The health and kingdom impact of our churches is directly connected to the health and vibrancy of our worship ministries.

So, how do we serve in the role of "The Enemy of Distraction"?

What Then Shall We Do?

There are four major areas of focus leaders can use to lead a ministry to avoid unnecessary distractions. These are areas in which the leader can provide structure and accountability to foster a healthy, disciple-making ministry.

1. Personal Spiritual Health
2. Congregational Responsibility

3. Development of Craft and Skills
4. Preparation for Service

Here are a few practical suggestions of establishing this value in your ministry:

Personal Spiritual Health

- Establish a routine of Bible study, prayer, and testimony in rehearsals and retreats with the leaders of your worship ministry.
- Use study materials with your teams—read books together, study Scripture together, have prayer times together.
- Create a spiritual culture that acknowledges to all the conviction that growth in godliness is a requirement of all leaders.

Congregational Responsibility

- Articulate the expectation that all leaders will be fully involved in small group Bible study, discipleship, and the ongoing mission efforts of the church. No "music only" leaders.

- Insist your musicians actively participate in worship gatherings, small groups, mission trips, etc., even when they are not leading.
- Directly connect the worship ministry with the preaching ministry of the church. Require musicians to be active listeners to the preaching ministry and consistently interact with the preaching themes of the pastor.
- Expect featured musicians/soloists to also participate in the larger ministry opportunities first.

Development of Craft and Skills

- Challenge leaders (including yourself) to work on their musical craft personally.
- Provide training opportunities for leaders for the skills used in worship.
- Invest in training tools and expect leaders to take advantage of them.
- Challenge your musicians to grow in their musical/technical skills with greater assignments.

Preparation for Service

- Expect all leaders to come to the worship gathering prepared.
- Musicians should know their music well and should have worked on it ahead of time.
- Technical operators have all the gear/visuals/lights ready to go.
- Individuals have prayed and prepared spiritually to lead and serve.

Setting up a culture that eliminates distractions will take time—whether you have been at the church for years, or are just beginning. But it is a necessary value for churches whose desire is to have healthy worship ministries.

Leaders first have to embody these values. Pray that God will allow you to see problems and grant you wisdom to address them in a loving and nurturing way. It may start with a simple plan like this:

1. Regularly articulate your desire to eliminate distractions that will affect how the gospel is presented through your ministry. Begin by giving your people the "why."

2. Make excellence your goal in everything—technical systems, musical presentations, team accountability—and prepare your people so that it is achievable.
3. Develop and maintain personal relationships with the team so that you will have the relational equity to address concerns when necessary.
4. Proactively communicate your expectations of team members regarding their use of social media, behavior, ministry participation, and the like.
5. Establish a dress code and enforce it. (Men—I highly recommend you enlist a trusted woman to communicate with the women in your ministry about concerns.)
6. Consider your responsibility to lead more important than your popularity among the team.
7. Seek godly council from your pastor or others when you have difficult situations to address.
8. Pray about existing distractions and how to deal with them.

Whatever title you may want to give the role of leading worship through music, because of all that is at stake, consider adding this one to the list:

We are "The Enemies of Distraction."

CHAPTER TEN

THE EZRA GENERATION

Every church leader desires to have a vibrant and healthy worship ministry in their church—a culture where people are engaged, developed, inspired, and encouraged through participation in the corporate worship of God's people.

These ministries faithfully tell the story of Jesus. They use their relationships and influence to develop lifelong disciples of Christ. They are churches that have a "come and worship" approach rather than a "come and watch worship" approach. They aspire for excellence, but with purpose, and every decision they make is intended to move the body of believers toward the realization of that purpose. Most of all, they aspire for the worship in their church to be focused on much more important things than music styles and song choices.

They want far more than just a well-oiled worship machine loaded with talented artists. They long for this ministry to be defined by more than just an absence of conflict; they deeply desire that the worship in their church reflect the biblical value of worship in the everyday lives of their people.

Christian artist Anthony Evans sings a powerful prayer in a song titled "See You Again." Here is the chorus of this poignant message:

> *Oh come, Lord, like a rushing wind*
> *We are desperate, for Your presence*
> *Revive us, by Your spirit within*
> *We want to see You again*
> *See You again!*[18]

This prayer is the aspiration of healthy churches in worship.

It Has Happened Before

There was a particular time early in the history of God's people when their worship was broken. They had been through the judgment and consequence of their sin and had lost their opportunity to meet with their God through worship as God allowed a conqueror to take them into bondage.

It was 587 BC, and Israel was taken into captivity to Babylon. Eventually, they cried out to the Lord in their brokenness and God heard them. In a second wave of returning exiles, God called a leader to bring a number of them back to the place of worship, repair the broken temple, and then lead the procession of praise into the house of God. The leader was a man named Ezra.

Thirteen years later, Nehemiah would return to repair the walls of Jerusalem. At the completion of the task, the people gathered at the Water Gate to worship God. It was Ezra who stepped forward with the word of God, and the worship that followed restored the right relationship of God to his people.

I'm asking God to do it again.

We Need Leaders

It will take a new generation of leaders aspiring to be used by God to move the church into biblical models of worship. These are leaders who know that the hand of God is resting on their lives.

Ezra was such a leader. The Bible tells the story of his life and the qualities of it that brought God's hand of grace to rest on his ministry.

It was a study of the book of Nehemiah that first piqued my interest in the scribe and priest, Ezra. The eighth chapter of this remarkable story is one of the most illustrative examples of worship in the entire Bible. When examining that text, we can easily see the role Ezra played in this amazing moment of worship.

Let's take a look at this scribe and priest to see what kind of man inspired a nation that had lost the joy of worshipping their God to come home to their Creator—and how the aspiration to worship God can change everything for the people of God.

Ezra was a descendant of the tribe of Judah and of Aaron through Eleazar. During his captivity in Babylon, Ezra was trained in the law as well as serving as a priest in the heralded priestly line of Aaron. Much like Nehemiah, Ezra earned the favor and trust of King Artaxerxes and received letters from the king granting him civil authority, along with the priestly authority he already possessed. Simply stated, Ezra was trained, knowledgeable, and trustworthy. He had lived so distinctively that he earned a dual leadership role in civil and religious government.

Ezra was an important contributor to the law as a scribe and teacher. Some ancient sources describe Ezra as instrumental in editing and standardizing the text of the Pentateuch, modernizing the language and establishing standards of expression. Many believe Ezra not only wrote the books of Ezra and Nehemiah, but also First and Second Chronicles, making him one of the most prolific writers of the Old Testament.

But he did more than write about God.

Ezra was a man of action. As he studied the law and copied it over and over as a scribe, something happened in the heart of this man that made him want more than to simply know the law—he wanted to know the God of the law. As a result, he determined to live his life by the prescriptions of his God.

Could it be that while he chronicled the slaying of Goliath, he understood for himself the power in the name of God? Was it in the retelling of the exodus of God's people that he first saw the faithfulness of Jehovah? Could he have believed, as he rewrote the story of God providing the sacrifice in Genesis 22 for Abraham and his son, that God would also make provision for his people in Babylon?

I believe the answer is "yes."

Ezra served a God he knew—a God who proved over and over again he loved his people and would keep his promises. So, when Nehemiah and Ezra stood before the people in Nehemiah 8, I believe Ezra had a sense that the God of the history he knew so well and loved would also meet his people in the here and now. I believe Ezra is one of those "unnamed" heroes of Hebrews 11 who were "approved by their faith" though they "did not receive what was promised" and is now in that "large cloud of witnesses" described in Hebrews 12:1. He loved God, loved his Word, and loved his people.

Study, Obey, and Teach

Ezra's life is a clear example of the three-step discipleship process of following after God. His example is outlined in Ezra 7:9b–10. It reads:

> . . . the gracious hand of his God was on him. Now Ezra had determined in his heart to study the law of the LORD, obey it, and teach its statutes and ordinances in Israel.

Mark it down.

Study

A person first, through God's Word, comes to an understanding of who God is and what he requires for relationship with him. By definition, that truth is exclusive—if it weren't, it wouldn't be true. When that awareness comes, a person can accept God's terms by confessing their need for a Savior and surrendering their lives to Messiah, or by rejecting his truth and walking away. And those are the only two options man has, no matter what our world wants us to believe.

Obey

Ezra studied God's law—the "word." This was the first step in the discipleship process. Then he obeyed what it said—the second step in the process. We call this "worship."

Worship as it is described in the Bible is not just demonstrating outward expressions of praise or song; worship is responding to God's Word expressed in Christ by submission and obedience in doing what Jesus said. Expressions of praise through song are only one aspect of worship.

Teach

Though Ezra could not have the full view of how Jesus would fulfill the law, he studied it and trusted that God would come through on his promises. Ezra placed his faith in God and responded in a life of obedience—true worship (Rom. 12:1). The third step comes in the last phrase of verse 10: "He taught its ordinances in Israel." There it is—Ezra's mission.

For our worship cultures to be healthy, our churches need leaders like Ezra who are committed to all three of these steps, in this order. It's a tall task. In fact, the Bible warns us against taking on teaching lightly (James 3:1). Nonetheless, it is a beautiful task, and God will equip those whom he calls. I believe he's calling a generation of Ezras.

A Modern-Day Ezra

Walking from East to West is the story of the life of Ravi Zacharias. It is the remarkable account of how this beloved Christian apologist and preacher of the gospel traversed the cultural complexities of faith from a boyhood filled with questions and doubt. This journey carried him to the halls of academia where today he often stands to defend his faith around the world. In the chapter titled "A Book on the Ash Heap," he recounts how a verse from a Bible given to his mother for him brought all the seeds of truth sown into his life together at a time when he needed it most. It was John 14:19b—"Because I live, you will live too."

His faith in God sprouted from the truth of God's Word.

The book goes on to describe how his life slowly turned toward ministry—winning a preaching contest, moving to Canada, and eventually becoming a teacher at Trinity Evangelical Divinity School, all the while studying and obeying the precepts of God's Word. One day, God prompts him to begin Ravi Zacharias International Ministries (RZIM), the outreach organization of his ministry.

Ravi has a story like Ezra's. After developing his understanding of God's Word and adhering to God's principles in the way he lived, Ravi discovered and embraced the mission of his life—a mission that drives him today.

God's Word produces worship in the heart of the believer that is marked by obedience, and that leads to a mission in life, just like Ezra.

There are dangers that come when we get these out of order. When mission precedes worship, it creates the dangerous environment of misplaced priorities. And when worship precedes the Word, well, it's not really true worship at all; it creates the very real possibility of heresy and idolatry.

The order is critical—God's Word, our response of worship, and our mission all flow together, in that order, over and over again.

What Do the Psalms Have to Do with It?

Many scholars agree that more than one person assembled the book of Psalms over time. The contributors to the Psalter are many and, though we know some of the authors, many of the psalms are anonymous.

But there is little doubt the likely editor of the last and longest portion of the Psalms, Book Five (Psalms 107–150) was Ezra. Why would this scribe, priest, and captain of the second wave of exiles returning to Jerusalem bother with the hymnbook?

It was because of the critical role that the spiritual discipline of worship has in the life of God's people. Rebuilding the walls would not have been enough to restore the rightful relationship of Israel and Jehovah. They had to rebuild their hearts in worship first.

Tomorrow's Worship Leaders

After thirty-five years of leading worship ministries in a variety of contexts, I've made a few observations about the "worship wars" era we have seen over the last several years. For the last thirteen of those years, I've had the perspective of serving churches in worship ministry through LifeWay Christian Resources. Emerging generations approach worship very differently than previous ones, and it's very different from the way my generation approached worship.

First, a little history.

In 1979, when I graduated high school, Christian radio was in its infancy. I'll never forget the first time I heard the classic Imperials song "Praise the Lord" on the radio. I had to pull over to the side of the road as Russ Taff sang, "When you're up against a struggle . . ." and weep. To think that a song written in the style of my youthful musical tastes could carry such a strong message about the Lord I loved was almost too much for me to comprehend.

Over the next twenty years, the music of Christian radio started an inevitable migration into the worship services of our churches.

A little later, a college football coach had a vision from the Lord—a vision of football stadiums that were filled up on Saturdays with energy and enthusiasm over football, filling up instead for a weekend with men to worship Jesus. They came from all racial and social circles and backgrounds. They came by the busload from churches of every kind, eager to worship God, and to challenge each other as husbands and fathers. By the early 1990s, tens of thousands of men were gathering in football stadiums across the country for these events called "Promise Keepers." Of the many men I know that attended one of those conferences (I attended several myself), almost none of them talk about the messages they heard. They remember the worship they experienced. There is something about the sound of 60,000 men singing that makes an impression on you.

But an interesting thing happened at those conferences. The worship was so powerful and expressive that many of those men went back to their churches and asked, "Why don't we have worship like that in our services?" Some wrongfully assumed it was the songs themselves that produced those experiences, so they began to explore those kinds of worship songs in their churches. Don't misunderstand, I believe God did use those songs, but the idea that the songs made the difference is a misunderstanding of worship.

Christian radio and Promise Keepers were just two factors of many that began the movement of modern worship songs migrating into our worship services. Between 1990 and 2000, most churches were affected in some way by these changes, some with great harm to the fellowship of believers. Many believers my age or older can tell some version of that story.

Today's younger generations are over it. They've heard all the new ways to express worship musically and, honestly, they're not that impressed. As they grew up watching the church get better and more expressive at worship, they were also watching the church become divided over worship styles and weaker in her impact on the world. They don't always get the same goose bumps at the key changes in the vertical songs that my generation valued so much. What is the answer? I believe it is a generation of Ezras leading worship in our churches.

When I think about an "Ezra generation" worship leader, I think about Aaron Keyes.

Aaron is a worship leader, songwriter, and artist. These days he is heavily involved in a movement called "10,000 Fathers." They clearly state their purpose is "Nurturing worship leaders who lead songs into pastors who lead people."

I'll never forget the first time I met him. I was at the Mission: Worship conference in Eastbourne on the southern coast of England. I was having a spot of tea with my good friend and Kingsway producer John Hartley when Aaron walked up. At first glance I thought, *This guy is an artist, great hair and all.* He looked like he was headed for a photo shoot for his next record. John introduced us and that was about all that was said until later that night.

After the evening worship time, Aaron invited me to join him and a few friends for dinner at a local restaurant. He and I happened to be seated on the same end of the table and the conversation began. Over two hours later, the owner of the establishment finally asked us to leave, since they had been closed for thirty minutes.

Aaron and I were talking about worship discipleship, a term I've come to use to describe our mission at LifeWay Worship. As we were exchanging Scriptures and questions, it wasn't long before we were finishing each other's sentences. It seems that Aaron was on his own journey of studying, obeying, and teaching God's law in the context of worship ministry. I was so encouraged and challenged by my time with him. He was one of those next-generation musicians who gave me hope that God is raising up a new kind of worship leader.

Since then, I've seen many more like him. In my own observation, this generation wants more depth and theology in their worship songs, more

Scripture, and more real-life application in authentic worship expressions. They want to do more than sing cool songs—they want to worship from the heart. And because this group is more concerned about biblical truth informing their expressions of worship, they connect to their mission much faster. They want to hear God's Word, obey it, worship him, and then get on mission—just like Ezra.

Going Back to School

I love to hang around college students.

For the last ten years, I have had the privilege of teaching in the School of Music and Worship at Liberty University. The experience has changed my life and helped me find what has become a major focus of my energy these days. The first time I realized how this generation could lead us back to a place of renewal in worship came during a lecture at Liberty.

I had led a class of about 150 students in a review of Nehemiah 8 and the role Ezra had in leading the worship that day. I went on to identify the marks of Ezra's life and the ways God uniquely prepared him for the task. I continued by calling out those same attributes in this generation that mark the life of the priest and scribe Ezra. And then, something came out of my mouth that surprised even me.

I felt the presence of God in that room and said with a conviction beyond my own confidence, "You are the Ezra Generation. You are the generation that God will use to bring renewal and revival to his church in America."

And one by one, students began to stand up as if they were accepting this mantle that the Lord had laid out in front of them. They were acknowledging their desire for the "gracious hand of God" to rest on them as it had on Ezra.

Now, several years later, I believe it even more. Every time I stand in front of this generation, I issue the same challenge because I remain convinced that God allowed me to see what he was doing and wants me to call it out.

The qualifying attributes of this generation are these: the desire to study God's Word, the intent of obedience to what it says, and the willingness to teach its ordinances to families and communities of faith as worship leaders. Just like Ezra.

This value—aspiring with purpose—is found in healthy worship ministries that fight for what matters the most. They pursue excellence in order to eliminate distractions from the greatest purpose of all—leading the response of worship in a community of believers taking the gospel to the world.

CONCLUSION

The last major skirmish of the Battle of New Orleans was fought on January 8, 1815. It was an epic struggle as seventy-five hundred British soldiers attacked General Andrew Jackson and his army of forty-five hundred Americans. The battle was horrific, as nearly two thousand died in a little over thirty minutes of fighting.

And it should have never been fought.

The Treaty of Ghent had been signed two weeks before the battle, on Christmas Eve, ending the War of 1812, but word had not yet reached the British forces attacking New Orleans. The only identifiable result in the aftermath of the battle was the notoriety it garnered for Andrew Jackson—a notoriety that eventually won him the presidency.

Simply put, the Battle of New Orleans was a complete waste of those lives and resources for both countries. It should have never happened. In the same way, with even more important consequences, many churches have fought a war over worship that should never have taken place.

It's time for it to end.

It's time to stop the conflicts around worship that disrupt and distract our churches. It's time to call off the fighting over music styles and ministry approaches in music. There have been too many casualties, too many unnecessary divisions and skirmishes that have done nothing but weaken the effectiveness of churches in their communities and the world.

I think about those families in Britain who heard the war was over, only to learn later their sons and brothers died in a battle that didn't matter. I think about the eight Americans who died in the battle and how senseless it must have seemed to their fellow soldiers and families.

Even sadder, I think about those once thriving communities of faith that divided over the song choices of their worship services, or the families that came to blows when the choir stopped wearing choir robes or the organ was replaced. Even more subtle are the aftereffects in all of those churches that divide their congregation with multiple styles of worship.

And I think about Shawn.

Shawn was new in his faith, coming from a family that had not walked with the Lord as he was growing up. His musical skills and spiritual hunger brought him the opportunity to join the music staff of a great church. This church had a rich tradition of missions, evangelism, and music. He was an important part of the team preparing the instrumentalists each week in worship.

When a new worship pastor began to push the musical choices to a more aggressive style, emotions in the church ran high. There were Bible study classes that began to sit in the foyer during the music in protest. Anonymous notes started showing up in the offering plate. People were saying hurtful and critical things about the music. Pretty soon, it got to be personal. Shawn—with longer hair and a more youthful look—became the target of some of the harshest criticisms. It all became more than he could take, and eventually, Shawn left the church.

Today, he no longer uses his musical talents in worship. He has renounced his faith and completely given up on the Bible as the authority for his life. Occasionally he expresses his disillusionment on the Internet, baiting "Christians" to convince him that Jesus is real. The hurtful rejection of the people in the church where he served crushed his fledgling faith to the point that he was no longer interested in what they had to say about Jesus.

Shawn is a casualty of a war we shouldn't be fighting.

This story may not be as uncommon as we think. We will never know how many "Shawns" came to our churches only to walk away, not because the music wasn't the style they preferred, but because the "Christians" gathering for worship had no room for a worship expression outside of their own preferences.

I'm so glad Jesus didn't feel that way.

Here We Are Again

The church at Rome didn't fare much better back in Paul's day. In the fourteenth chapter of his letter to the church there, Paul identifies two issues that were threatening the unity of the church. The first one concerned whether or not meat should be eaten. The second was a question about whether or not a particular day of the week should be observed as more significant than the others.

First Corinthians 11 is similar. Paul addresses another concern that was causing issues in the fellowship at Corinth. It was a question about the appropriate attire for a woman in worship and whether or not her head should be covered when she was praying. (I can truthfully say, that particular one has never come up in any of the churches I've attended!)

In John 4, the Samaritan woman—once she realized Jesus was a prophet—asked a question about worship. It seems we have always had the tendency of disagreement when it comes to how we do church.

Perhaps the one thought that best summarizes the attitude of maturity when it comes to these kinds of issues is found in Romans 14:7—"For none of us lives for himself, and no one dies for himself."

The principle is this: for the sake of our sisters and brothers, we can choose to end the war over styles of ministry. It's time to focus on the essentials. It's time for believers to grow up in their faith and put an end to the unnecessary carnage of the worship wars.

We need leaders who understand this. We need followers of Jesus who love him and their fellow brothers and sisters more than their own preferences.

Here's what it boils down to. Would we rather win the argument? Or would we rather win our world? Because we won't win both.

Years ago, I saw a godly leader model this for me during a worship service. He was standing in what looked to be an almost protest posture—arms folded, mouth closed—during the singing. Yet, at the same time, he was obviously moved emotionally while the congregation sang the song. Later when I asked him about it, his reply stunned me: "I hate that song we were singing. As a matter of fact, I hate most of the music we do." But when I pressed him for the reason he was visibly moved, he continued, "But I love what God is doing in our church—the young families, the people engaged in worship. I thank God for what you are doing."

I replied, "So, let me get this straight—you hate what I do—but you love what God is doing through me?"

"Yep. That's about it," he said.

That looks a whole lot like Romans 14 to me.

We need to get over those things that divide us, those secondary issues that Romans 14 describes as "doubtful." We need to focus on a few essentials that will foster healthy congregations who hear

God, worship him in spirit and truth, and join the mission of making disciples and bringing many more worshippers along for the journey.

Tell the Story.

Make Disciples.

Engage the Body.

Aspire with Purpose.

The rest is just details.

NOTES

1. Mark Batterson, *Primal* (Colorado Springs: Multnomah, 2009), 5.

2. Mike Harland and Stan Moser, *Seven Words of Worship* (Nashville: B&H Publishing, 2008), 15.

3. Anne Graham Lotz, *I Saw the Lord* (Grand Rapids, MI: Zondervan, 2006), 147.

4. The event is chronicled in the *New York Times* article published 9/24/01 by Robert D. McFadden titled, "A Nation Challenged: The Service."

5. Eric Metaxas, *Bonhoeffer: Pastor, Martyr, Prophet, Spy* (Nashville: Thomas Nelson, 2010), 99.

6. Nik Ripken, *The Insanity of God* (Nashville: B&H, 2013), 299.

7. Ibid.

8. Zac Hicks, *The Worship Pastor* (Grand Rapids, MI: Zondervan, 2016), 175.

9. Ibid.

10. See *Baptist Hymnal* 2008, Hymn 232 and Hymn 506.

11. Copyright 2015, Sony/ATV Music Publishing, LLC, Warner/Chappell Music, Inc., Essential Music Publishing.

12. Keith and Kristyn Getty, *Sing! How Worship Transforms Your Life, Family, and Church* (Nashville: B&H Publishing, 2017), 89.

13. Stan Moser, *We Will Stand* (CCM United, 2015), 41.

14. Bob Kauflin, *True Worshippers* (Wheaton, IL: Crossway, 2015), 98.

15. Harold Best, *Unceasing Worship: Biblical Perspectives on Worship and the Arts* (Downers Grove, IL: InterVarsity Press, 2003), 47.

16. Ibid., 144–45.

17. David Regier, *Then Tweets My Soul: The Best of the Church Curmudgeon* (Moscow, ID: Canon Press, 2016), 103, 63, 37, 102.

18. Words and music by Krissy Nordhoff and Michael Neale. Copyright © 2014 Integrity's Praise! Music/Michael Neale Music & TwoNords Music.